The Lion and Lamb Initiative

Handbook for Rebuilding America the Good, the Great, and the Godly

Lawrence Paul Hebron

Table of Contents

Copyright.. 1

Dedication... 3

PART ONE:.. 5

CHAPTER ONE:.. 7

Discussion 11

CHAPTER TWO:... 13

Discussion 17

CHAPTER THREE: 19

Discussion 23

CHAPTER FOUR:.. 25

Discussion 41

CHAPTER FIVE:.. 45

Discussion 57

CHAPTER SIX:.. 59

Discussion 69

CHAPTER SEVEN: 73

Discussion 77

PART TWO:... 79

CHAPTER EIGHT:... 81

Discussion 83

CHAPTER NINE: 85

Discussion 91

CHAPTER TEN: 93

Discussion 101

CHAPTER ELEVEN: 105

Discussion 119

PART THREE: 123

CHAPTER TWELVE: 125

Discussion 133

CHAPTER THIRTEEN: 135

Discussion 141

CHAPTER FOURTEEN: 143

Discussion 153

CHAPTER FIFTEEN: 157

Discussion 159

CHAPTER SIXTEEN: 161

Discussion 165

CHAPTER SEVENTEEN: 167

Discussion 179

CHAPTER EIGHTEEN: 183

Discussion 185

CHAPTER NINETEEN: 187

Discussion 191

APPENDICES 193

APPENDIX A: 195

APPENDIX B: 199

APPENDIX C: 209

Copyright

The Lion and Lamb Initiative: Handbook for Rebuilding America the Good, the Great, and the Godly

Copyright © 2025 Lawrence Paul Hebron

(Defiance Press & Publishing, LLC)

Published by Defiance Press & Publishing, LLC

Bulk orders of this book may be obtained by contacting Defiance Press & Publishing, LLC. www.defiancepress.com.

Defiance Press & Publishing, LLC

281-581-9300

info@defiancepress.com

Dedication

THIS BOOK IS DEDICATED TO
GOD AND THE UNITED STATES OF AMERICA

With special appreciation to

Walter, Ena, Dori, Lisa, Heather, Joel, and Ryan

PART ONE:

In the Beginning

"In the beginning God created the heavens and the earth…"

Genesis 1:1

CHAPTER ONE:

Quo Vadis; Introduction

Americans don't agree about much any more. Tempers are rising, and the melting pot is boiling over. E pluribus unum (out of many, one) has become e unum pluribus (out of one, many). There is one dark and dire exception to this lack of consensus, however. Nearly everyone agrees that the nation is in trouble. As you might expect, we don't all agree on the source or nature of that trouble, but we all agree that the trouble is real.

Those on the Left see an existential threat to our democracy. Those on the Right see an existential threat to our republic. Beyond this, there are innumerable more specific problems, each eroding the foundation of our civil culture like the relentless waves that beat upon a coastal cliff—each corrupting our national fiber like voracious cancer cells. Immorality is idolized. Aberrant sexual practices are promoted and exalted. Crime is pervasive, and those entrusted to protect us from this are willfully failing. Sexual abuse, including of our children, is rampant. Pornography is readily available and widely consumed—even in school libraries. The use of dangerous drugs is growing while the government is legitimizing it. Family values are decaying and divorce has reached epidemic proportions. The slaughter of our most innocent and helpless children, for no better reason than convenience, has placed us in the company of mass-murderers like Hitler, Stalin, and Mao. America has become a moral toxic waste dump. History consistently shows that when great nations and cultures experience these trends without stopping them, their collapse is inevitable and imminent. So, what will be our fate—quo vadis—decline and death or revival and life? Furthermore, whom can we trust to lead the rebirth of America?

There is another dangerous trend to add to the list above, but this one may help us answer the question just posed. We have become grossly overly politicized. We look to the politicians and their parties to solve these problems and virtually all other problems as well. But didn't these problems happen under their watch—in fact, often with their collaboration? Does it make any sense to trust the problem-causers to be the problem-solvers? Of course not.

Think about it. We have not had a single president who was not a Democrat nor Republican since the 1850s—that's over a century-and-a-half. These same two parties have also dominated the national legislature and state governments as well. It would be difficult to place the blame for our national afflictions on anyone other than these two bands of scoundrels—and it seems that almost everyone knows it.

I have a brief homily that I have come to refer to as my "political mantra." It goes like this: "The government is corrupt. The political system is dysfunctional. Both political parties have not only failed us; they have betrayed us. We cannot trust them with our futures. We, the people, must take back control ourselves." For more than a decade-and-a-half I have repeated these exact words to Republicans, Democrats, independents, office-holders and candidates at all levels of government, party leaders, and average citizens. Can you guess how many have objected? Not one. Not one. Not long ago I was introduced to the chairman of a county central committee of one of the Big Two Parties. I recited my mantra and told him the results of the responses to it. I gave him the perfect opportunity to break my record—which you'd think he would be glad to do given his position of leadership in the party—but he did not. Like most others, the best he could say was that although his party wasn't perfect, it wasn't as bad as the other one. In effect, he justified loyalty to his party by arguing that it didn't stink as badly as the other guys. I think Americans deserve better than the least putrid option.

The Democrats and the Republicans have failed us. It would be foolish, even suicidal, to continue to trust them. The party politicians do not have solutions for our problems. They offer political cures for what are often moral maladies. A central premise of this book will be that we must seek moral solutions to those problems which have often been disguised as political or economic in nature. You cannot cure cancer by treating it like toenail fungus. Similarly, we cannot successfully treat America's diseases until we recognize their true cause. We need to learn the lesson that our Founders and Framers understood clearly. Charles Carroll, a signer of the Declaration of Independence, echoed the sentiment of many other luminaries in our early history when he wrote, "without morals a republic cannot subsist any length of time; they therefore who are decrying the Christian religion, whose morality is so sublime and pure...are undermining the solid foundation of morals, [which is] the best security for the duration of free governments."

John Adams understood this with crystal clarity. He wrote, "Our Constitution was made only for a moral and religious people. It is wholly inadequate to the government of any other." Well, if "Our Constitution was made only for a moral and religious people", what happens if we cease to be a moral and religious people? Our government fails.

We must acknowledge that the party politicians do not have solutions for our problems. They offer self-serving political cures for moral diseases. If we continue to follow them, the consequences will be disastrous. So, which way should we go, and what price are we willing to pay to save America?

The apocryphal book entitled *Acts of Peter* never made it into the Bible, but it tells a story that poses a question that is very relevant to us today. Saint Peter is fleeing Rome to avoid persecution. Things are not going well for Christians, and Peter wants to get out while the getting is still good. Of course, this will leave the remaining Christians without a great leader to do for them those things that great leaders do. On his way out of town, he sees Jesus approaching him, walking the same road but in the opposite direction. Peter asks, "Quo Vadis?", Latin for, "Where are you going?" Jesus pauses. He looks at Peter and says, "I am going to Rome to be crucified again." The old fisherman gets the message and is ashamed. The Master had already done far more than His share. The time had come for His followers to do theirs. And he did. Peter turned around and marched back to Rome, where he would be crucified, reportedly upside down.

Quo Vadis, Americans? The Founders and Framers of this nation paid an unimaginable price to secure our liberty and prosperity. I suspect they would be willing to return to do it again if they had to. But, why do they have to? Preserving, protecting, and defending America is our job now; and like Peter, we need to turn around and get to work.

Churches, synagogues, and other Godly organizations and people need to unite to address issues such as poverty, hunger, bigotry, injustice, homelessness, grief, addiction, crime, etc. The government should not be doing that which we should be doing for ourselves. And as the church grows, government can shrink, and freedom can increase. Instead of habitually turning to the elephant and the donkey, we must once again trust the Lion and the Lamb. The Christian Church, along with our Jewish allies, must take the lead in rebuilding America the good, the great, and the Godly. We must remember that America did not become great because of our government, but because of our God. The chapters which follow will detail why this is true and what we must do to save America.

Discussion

"Americans don't agree about much any more." Have you found this to be true? Why do you think there is so much divisiveness and division in the country?

"Nearly everyone agrees that the nation is in trouble."

What do you see as the greatest threats to the nation?

What needs to be done to reduce these threats?

"Those on the Left see an existential threat to our democracy. Those on the Right see an existential threat to our republic."

Did you know that our Founders and Framers did not want to create a democracy? For the most part, they disliked democracy, which some even referred to as "mobocracy." Throughout history, democracies have proved to be inherently unstable and subject to manipulation by powerful special interest groups. In a democracy, the will of 51% of the people determines policy. There is no stability. If 51% of the people vote for a right to free speech or religion or press one day, you have the right to these things. But if 51% of the people vote against these things the next day, you do not have the right to these things. In a republic, "lex rex", which means "the law is king." So, if the fundamental law of the land (Constitution) says you have the right to free speech or religion or press and 99% of the people vote against these things, the people still retain these rights. The Founders and Framers sought to create a democratic republic where the will of the people would always be expressed and would influence policy but could not prevail against a higher law, in our case, the Constitution.

Where would you rather live—a democracy or a republic?

"America has become a moral toxic waste dump." Do you agree with this? If so, give some examples to support this view.

"We have become grossly overly politicized. We look to the politicians and their parties to solve these problems and virtually all other problems as well. But didn't these problems happen under their watch—in fact, often with their collaboration? Does it make any sense to trust the problem-causers to be the problem-solvers?"

Do you agree that, as a nation, we are inclined to look to politicians and politics to solve most of our problems?

Do you agree that the politicians and politics are responsible for many of our problems? If so, give some examples.

The author refers to what he calls his "political mantra." It goes like this: *"The government is corrupt. The political system is dysfunctional. Both political parties have not only failed us; they have betrayed us. We cannot trust them with our futures. We, the people, must take back control ourselves."*

How do you feel about this—do you agree? If so, think of some examples of why you feel betrayed.

If we cannot trust politics and the politicians to solve our problems, where else can we turn?

John Adams wrote, *"Our Constitution was made only for a moral and religious people. It is wholly inadequate to the government of any other."*

Do you agree? Why does our Constitution require a moral and religious people in order to work?

"The government should not be doing that which we should be doing for ourselves."

What could go wrong if the government starts doing too much; namely, things "we should be doing for ourselves."

"We must remember that America did not become great because of our government, but because of our God."

Back in the early 1830s, Alexis de Tocqueville came here from France to study what was going on in this young country—the United States. He wrote that one of the things that struck him as unique about the American experience was the supportive relationship that existed between the government and the church. Do you believe that this helped set America apart from the rest of the world and helped pave the way for America's greatness?

CHAPTER TWO:

Apple Pies and Big Bangs

"If you wish to make an apple pie from scratch, you must first invent the universe." This is how the first paragraph of the ninth chapter of Carl Sagan's book, *Cosmos,* concludes. [Random House, 1980] That sounds a bit hyperbolic, but what else would you expect from a mathematician? The question is, "Is it true?" and "What is its relevance?"

According to the beliefs of most modern scientists, everything began some 13.8 billion years ago with a massive explosion of energy known as the Big Bang (Let there be light.) Energy emanated outward in all directions at the speed of light, or close to it. As strange as this was, it was just the beginning of strange things. Radiant energy began to congeal into tiny globs of matter called atoms, which is just energy in an other form. Simple atoms, which we have named "hydrogen" came into existence first, and in massive quantities. As these atoms came close enough to one another, another strange thing happened. An elemental force, which we have called "gravity", began to pull these atoms together. Once a sufficient number of them gathered close enough to each other, their combined energy caused these tiny orbs of hydrogen to ignite, radiating light and heat and some other strange things. We call these massive glowing balls of hydrogen "stars." This process was repeated trillions of times as the universe grew. The heat inside these stars was sufficient to cause some of these hydrogen atoms to fuse together into a larger atom we have named "helium." Eventually, the hydrogen fuel of the stars burned up leading to the death of the stars, but they did not all die in the same manner. Some exploded. Some cooled and swelled—their gravity no longer sufficient to hold them in a compact sphere. Others went the other way, having so much mass that the surviving matter of the dying star was pulled by the overwhelming gravitational force of the enormous quantity of hydrogen to shrink into a super-dense mass we have called "black holes." Lots of strange stuff was going on.

These stellar furnaces caused even heavier atoms than helium to be created. All of the left over "ash" of these dead stars was discharged into the cosmos where the process would start all over again. New masses of atoms would be drawn together by gravity, ignite, and burn for very long times. And even heavier atoms would be created in the process. After a few generations of this, we had all the types of atoms included on what we call the periodic table of the elements. And with all this diversity, new forms of structures other than gassy stars could form, including rocky planets. And then something really strange happened: life. The universe was no longer inanimate. Somehow, atoms started to form little clubs which became what we call cells which ultimately became plants and animals. These clubs interacted with other liquids and gasses and solids in their vicinity and grew larger and more diverse. We got sugars and grains and fruits. And eventually, another type of club, called animals, developed and learned how to live off the plants and other animals around them. One of these animals even learned how to turn those sugars and grains and fruits into apple pies. But none of this would be possible had the universe not first been created. So we, like Sagan, must come to the conclusion that, "If you wish to make an apple pie from scratch, you must first invent the universe."

All of this is quite remarkable, until you start to really think about it—and then it becomes remarkably, staggeringly, incredibly, stunningly, mind-boggling. One of those staggering realizations is that we all are made of "star-stuff", as Sagan, himself, points out much earlier in his book. If the scientists are right, then every one of the 17 to 36 trillion cell in your body (depending on whether you are a child, an adult, female, or male) were made in stars that existed billions of years ago and trillions of miles away—and likely different stars at that! That makes each of us pretty special. Oh, but it gets much more remarkable than that. To illustrate why, I must shift gears from the realm of physical science to that of spiritual theology. I must set aside *Cosmos* and pick up the *Bible*.

* * *

"In the beginning God created the heavens and the earth." [Genesis 1:1] And so begins the famous Biblical account of the Creation. As is the case with the physical scientists' account of creation, there are some pretty strange things going on in the Biblical account as well. Here, I will only point out one.

In the beginning God created the heavens and the earth. Okay. Out of what? Presumably, at that time there was only God and nothing else. So, what did He use to make everything?

Like many other young marrieds, my wife and I did not have much money. Nearly all the few items of furniture we did have in our home were either hand-me-downs or borrowed, and pretty meager at that. Our black-and-white television sat atop a wobbly card table. We needed more furniture, but didn't have the money to buy it. Something occurred to me. For about the same money it would cost to buy a coffee table, for example, I could buy some power tools and materials and make the coffee table—and I would still have the tools to make more furniture. And that's what I did. I decided on a rustic style for my first project, the aforementioned coffee table. Given my level of skill, that poor table was going to look "rustic" no matter what, so why not just go with the flow? Now that I had the tools, I went to the hardware store and bought the materials I needed. Notice the inescapable conclusion; namely, no building materials, no table. Now, back to the Biblical account of the Creation.

If, before the beginning, there was nothing but God, then what did He use to make everything? He couldn't just pop over to the Creation Depot and buy a gajillion tons of atoms and some very large tools. There was nothing but Him, which leads me to the inescapable conclusion that He made everything out of Himself.

Actually, this fits nicely with the current assumptions of modern scientists. For well over a century, scientists have accepted the belief that everything is energy. Actually, Albert Einstein said exactly that. The Bible tells us that God is Spirit. [John 4:24] Spirit is a form of energy. So, it sure looks like God (Spirit/Energy) made everything (energy) out of Himself (Energy). And if that is true, then we are not just "star-stuff", we are "God-stuff." And when you start to consider the implications of that, it is infinitely more than merely remarkably, staggeringly, incredibly, stunningly, mind-boggling.

In the next chapter, we will start to consider a very powerful consequence of this revelation; namely, how to solve just about every inter- and intra-personal problem.

Discussion

"If, before the beginning, there was nothing but God, then what did He use to make everything?...There was nothing but Him, which leads me to the inescapable conclusion that He made everything out of Himself."

The author was led to the "inescapable conclusion" that God made everything out of Himself. Can you come to another conclusion? Theologians, pastors, and priests often talk about how God "spoke" everything into existence. Well, sort of. We see a recurring pattern in the first chapter of Genesis where God said something, and it happened. "God said, 'Let there be light,' and there was light." "God said, 'Let there be an expanse between the waters to separate water from water.'" "God said..." and so forth. But even if we take this literally, it is not an alternative to the idea that God made everything out of Himself. When you speak, your lungs contract forcing air over your vocal cords which is further altered by your mouth. You created the sound waves (energy) which go out to influence the world around you and create new realities. Speaking comes from within you, whether You are God or you are a sapient primate. So, we are still left with the question, "Can you come to another conclusion" about where God got the stuff He used to make everything?

If God made everything out of Himself, then we are not merely "star-stuff" as Sagan wrote, we are "God-stuff." How does that make you feel?

If you are made of "God-stuff", and if God is good, then why do you do bad things?

Do you feel you are living up to your potential? If not, why not, and what are you going to do about it?

CHAPTER THREE:

Toward a Spiritual Theory of

Everything

The physicists have something they call a Theory of Everything (TOE), which is a hypothetical, unified, all-encompassing, final, theoretical framework of physics that allegedly fully explains and links together all aspects of the universe. Perhaps it's time for us to do something akin to this in the spiritual realm.

If God exists, and if He created everything, and if there was nothing but Him when He did this, then it follows that He must have made everything out of Himself. Accordingly, everything, including us, is made of God-stuff. And this means that everything has a God-nature.

If you make a cake with chocolate, it will have a chocolate nature. It won't look or taste or smell like vanilla or strawberries or cinnamon. It will look and taste and smell like chocolate. If you make a Creation out of God, it will have a God nature. Every galaxy, every star, every planet, every plant, every animal, every cell will not only reflect God, they will radiate God. They have to. That is what they are made of. A chocolate cake cannot taste like cinnamon. "The heavens declare the glory of God; and the firmament sheweth his handywork." [Psalm 19:1, KJV] Similarly, every galaxy, star, planet, plant, animal, and cell is connected to God through a universal tapestry of energy. Furthermore, every galaxy, star, planet, plant, animal, and cell can only fulfill its true purpose and realize its destiny as long as it stays connected with God and follows the will of God. That is not a problem for most of these items. They have no free will, so they cannot wander off from the Godly way. There is at least one significant exception to this: us. For whatever His reasons, God allowed us the freedom to wander off His pathways, and boy did we wander. Through sin (disobedience to the will and law of God) we broke the connection with Him which, in turn, prevented us from fulfilling our true purpose and realizing our intended destinies. That spoiled everything. Even though we usually rebel against God because we think we will find something more satisfying along a different pathway, it never works out. Never. A being must live in accordance with its nature or its existence will be unnatural and unfulfilling—even fatal. A bird cannot live as a fish; nor a fish like a bird. A bird and a fish can only realize their best life as long as they stay true to the nature God gave them. The same is true for us.

Why is there suffering and injustice and depression and afflictions and grief and woe and agonies of all manner? Trace these manifestations of misery back to the root cause and you almost always find they started with an offense against God's will. When we detach ourselves from God and deny our Godly nature, bad things always happen. Always. A conversation I recently had with a researcher illustrates this. It has to do with the cause of homosexuality.

I don't know if we could find something that is more vehemently condemned in the Bible than homosexual behavior. It is described as detestable, abhorrent, and an abomination. The spiritually unsophisticated are quick to claim that the God of the Bible hates homosexuals. No! He loves them. What He hates is what caused this perversion in the first place and how it robs His children of the life and joy He intends for them.

The researcher I met recently told me about his findings regarding the cause of homosexuality which began with some undercover work at a "Gay Bar" in southern California. Under the guise of just striking up a conversation with many of the patrons of the bar, he steered the discussion to the matter of the cause of homosexuality. "Do you think you were born that way?" he asked. The nearly universal response surprised him and led to further research. No, they didn't think they were born that way. In almost every case, they had been sexually abused, usually at an early age. It was the abuse, and how they chose to respond to it, that led to them adopting a homosexual lifestyle. Think about that. If these children had never been treated in an ungodly manner, they never would have turned to the kind of lifestyle that denies them the joy and fulfillment God intends through a normal family life. Now, I'm not saying that all cases of homosexuality result from this single source; but it made me wonder if perhaps many other kinds of personal and social aberrant behavior might also be spawned by abuse and the reaction to it.

It has become commonplace in modern America for people with "traditional values"—usually encompassing Christianity and patriotism—to describe much of what is being advocated and implemented by those who do not share these same values, as "crazy." Actually, I don't think it is crazy. I think everything makes sense—from a certain perspective. Even the behavior of that "crazy" guy pushing a shopping cart filled with trash down the street wearing eight layers of clothes when it is 105 degrees while doing his dance and shouting at the Devil makes sense—to him. And if we could get inside his head, we'd realize why that behavior makes sense to him. This actually proves to be a very powerful analytical tool. Whenever a proposal or cause of action seems nonsensical, reverse-engineer it. Ask yourself, "From what basic assumptions or objectives does this make sense?" I suspect that in most cases, we will find that the "craziness" was engendered by abuse. Let me illustrate with two examples.

First example: During the summer between fourth and fifth grades, my parents moved, and I started attending a different school. One of my new classmates was an especially disagreeable fellow I'll call "Don." Don was always in trouble, usually for fighting. He was very violent. A couple years later we went to different schools, and I didn't see him again until my senior year of high school, 1968—1969. Don now presented himself as a peacenik. The war in Vietnam was at its peak, and Don had joined the small group of anti-war demonstrators on campus. I didn't buy it. The leopard doesn't change its spots, and I didn't think it was likely that Don had become a pacifist. Sure enough, before the school year had ended, Don was talking about "killing the pigs"; that is, the police. That was more like the Don we all knew and disliked. But how does this behavior make any sense? You'd think Don would be the first to enlist in the armed forces so he could go overseas and kill a bunch of people without getting in trouble.

Second example: Many of our modern radicals make a point of sympathizing with Islam, especially when it comes to opposing Israel. These same people, however, also often are rabid supporters of the LGBTQ+ movement. How does that make any sense? Christian, Jewish, and Muslim theology all condemn homosexual behavior, but the Muslims are about the only ones currently doing anything about it. Convicted homosexuals are often executed in Islamic nations, occasionally by casting them off tall buildings. You'd think the leftist wokesters would either condemn Islam or condemn LGBTQ+ or condemn them both, but not embrace them both. How does this make any sense? It doesn't. Unless….

Some people are driven by a righteous obsession to know the truth. That obsession often leads them to uncomfortable conclusions, but they would rather know and honor the truth than be comfortable. Other people are driven by an infernal obsession to promote an ideology. That obsession often leads them to obvious and foolhardy inconsistencies, but they would rather protect their ideology than be consistent. So, what motivates this second group? Clearly, the ideology serves some purpose that is important to them; and when it comes to the leftist wokesters, that purpose seems to be a personal desire to spit in the face of the authorities. That's why they hate America. That's why they topple statues of our heroes. That's why they spray graffiti on our monuments. That's why they desecrate churches. That's why they burn the flag. That's why they destroy businesses. That's why they shout obscenities at those who stand for God and country. But why do they want to spit in the face of the authorities? My suspicion is that the authorities (parents, teachers, law enforcers, bosses, etc.) have wounded them—perhaps in an abusive way—at some point. They want to strike back, but the authorities are too powerful, so they redirect their vengeance and rage into something they can pull off, like denigrating those things the authorities hold in reverence and respect. I suspect that is also what happened to Don. At some point he was abused by someone he could not strike back at (probably his parents), and so he diverted his violence against his classmates which embarrassed his parents.

The point of this argument is simply this: if people had not treated others in an ungodly manner in the first place, a vast majority of the violence and hatred and anti-social behavior we have experienced would never have happened. Across the board, life would be so much better—personally, socially, politically, economically, spiritually. If we want to make things better, we must embrace our Godly natures. Reform and joy do not emanate from the elephant and the donkey. They come from the Lion and the Lamb. This must be the focus of our rebirth. This is how we will save America. We must return to God and once again embrace our Godly natures. Can this be done? Of course! How can I be so confident? Because we have already done it. What I propose is nothing new. It is nothing we must create. It is something we must remember and recreate. Let's see.

Discussion

If everything is made of God-stuff, then *"Every galaxy, every star, every planet, every plant, every animal, every cell will not only reflect God, they will radiate God. They have to. That is what they are made of... Furthermore, every galaxy, star, planet, plant, animal, and cell can only fulfill its true purpose and realize its destiny as long as it stays connected with God and follows the will of God... A being must live in accordance with its nature or its existence will be unnatural and unfulfilling—even fatal."*

Do you feel there is something missing or defective in your life? Have you listened to the self-help advice offered by various "experts" and yet you still feel something is missing? Could it be that you are not embracing your true Godly nature?

"Why is there suffering and injustice and depression and afflictions and grief and woe and agonies of all manner? Trace these manifestations of misery back to the root cause and you almost always find they started with an offense against God's will."

Think about some things (other than a physical injury or illness) that afflict you; that is, cause you suffering, grief, woe, etc. Now, trace them back to the thing that caused these. Did they involve "an offense against God's will"?

Would you be better off if that offense had not happened?

The author writes about a conversation he had with a researcher who concluded that *"In almost every case, they* [homosexuals] *had been sexually abused, usually at an early age. It was the abuse, and how they chose to respond to it, that led to them adopting a homosexual lifestyle."* If that is true, then is it truly helpful and compassionate to encourage homosexuals to remain in such a lifestyle? We even go so far as to celebrate and take pride in this aberrant behavior. If this behavior is the result of abuse and denies homosexuals a lifestyle that would genuinely bless them, wouldn't the compassionate thing be to help them understand the origins of their behavior so they could abandon it?

The author writes that *"if people had not treated others in an ungodly manner in the first place, a vast majority of the violence and hatred and anti-social behavior we have experienced would never have happened. Across the board, life would be so much better—personally, socially, politically, economically, spiritually. If we want to make things better, we must embrace our Godly natures."* Do you agree? If not, what explanation do you have for the woes of individuals and societies?

The easy answer to the last question is that we are a fallen race. Okay, but doesn't that ultimately get back to us abandoning our Godly nature and turning from God?

The author continues that *"Reform and joy do not emanate from the elephant and the donkey. They come from the Lion and the Lamb. This must be the focus of our rebirth. This is how we will save America."* There have been a number of "Spiritual Awakenings" in American history. Generally, they worked to put America back on the right track by returning the people's focus to God and His way. Do you think this is necessary now?

CHAPTER FOUR:

In The Beginning—American

Genesis

"In the beginning God created the heavens and the earth. And the earth was without form, and void; and darkness was upon the face of the deep. And the Spirit of God moved upon the face of the waters." [Genesis 1:1-2]

It often takes years before a fruit tree will bear any fruit. Until it does, it may be difficult to know what kind of tree is growing in the orchard—unless you know what kind of seeds were planted there. Beginnings yield consequences as well as explanations. If you know how a tree starts, you will not only know what kind of fruit it will bear, you also will know how to nurture that tree so it will bear much fruit. The same applies to nations. Let us briefly explore the genesis of America.

Many will think that this brief history is unnecessary. Perhaps you are one of them. You may think you could skip this because you already know enough about the essential history of America's beginning. No, you do not. Our formal educational system—exemplified in our network of public, government run schools—has lied to us for decades. It has had reason to do so, and that reason has nothing to do with what is best for America and its people. For example, a few months ago I talked with a family that included three school-age children. During the course of that conversation, the daughter, who attended a public middle school, said that "the only thing they teach us about George Washington is that he was a racist slaveowner." This is an injustice of incalculable magnitude, as we will see in a later chapter. This representation of the "indispensable man" does, however, serve a particular purpose which, I just noted, has nothing to do with what is best for America and its people. Let us now confront some important and necessary aspects of our history, and let us begin at the beginning.

The Finding and Founding of America

The modern discovery and development of the Americas was initiated by Christopher Columbus' famous journey in 1492. True, Scandinavians arrived in North America centuries before Columbus, but their efforts left little lingering effect other than to give archeologists and anthropologists uncomfortably chilly places to excavate.

What do we know about Columbus' motivation for setting his sails to lead him into an uncertain future on the Sea of Darkness, as the Atlantic was known? Well, establishment educational institutions and their archives describe him as a daring explorer, a greedy merchant, a prideful sea captain, and the harbinger of colonialism. That all sounds very egocentric, doesn't it? No room there for any humanitarianism nor any other noble motive for that matter. However, any conscientious and responsible examination must, of course, include Columbus' own assessment. Is that how he saw it?

Columbus attests in his personal log that his purpose in seeking "undiscovered worlds" was to, "bring the Gospel of Jesus Christ to the heathens" and to "bring the Word of God to unknown coastlands." Now, some of our inveterate whiners, predisposed to find offense in any utterance, may object to descriptions such as "heathens"; but keep in mind that the pejorative connotation applied by modern users of the term was not so commonplace back then. Still others may find his remarks dripping in religious and cultural imperialism. Perhaps, but I think a more warmhearted motivation may also lie at the root of Columbus' remark.

Washington Irving is probably best known for his book, *The Legend of Sleepy Hollow*, but he had many other credits as well. He was a diplomat (U.S. ambassador to Spain from 1842—1846), biographer, and historian. Among other subjects, he studied Christopher Columbus, and had this to say about him, "Columbus came as a religious man, an admiral of Christ, to find the continent, not for its material treasures, but because it held souls which he wished to bring as a trophy to the feet of Christ." Perhaps that should not be surprising from someone whose first name means "Christ bearer." Still, the habitually offended may find something deeply sinister in his motives; namely, forcibly imposing one's own religious tenets on others. To the contrary, Columbus believed the best gift that could be given to anyone was a loving relationship with Jesus, and that, it seems, is exactly what he intended.

He christened the first island upon which he landed "San Salvador", which means "Holy Savior." Shortly after coming ashore, Columbus knelt and prayed these words: "O Lord, Almighty and everlasting God, by Thy holy Word Thou hast created the heaven and the earth, and the sea; blessed and glorified be Thy Name, and praised be Thy Majesty, which hath deigned to use us, Thy humble servants, that Thy holy Name may be proclaimed in this second part of the earth." He then ordered his men to erect a large wooden cross, "As a token of Jesus Christ our Lord, and in honor of the Christian faith." He continued this practice every time they landed on a new island.

The modern discovery of the Americas was motivated by a desire to "go and make disciples of all nations…." [Matthew 28:19] That motivation continued through the settlement of a string of British colonies along the eastern seaboard of North America.

The British Colonies

If you consult the tomes of modern, establishment education, you likely will be misinformed to believe that the founding of the original British colonies in the Americas was an imperialist venture motivated by a spirit of military expansion and economic enrichment. Unarguably, these were important considerations, but were they the only ones? Were they even the principal ones? Let's see.

Spain, one of Britain's main rivals, was making deep advances in the Americas, especially in the south. France, another British competitor, was tinkering about in the north. This left some acreage available in between, and the British decided they had better get busy. Their first attempt at a permanent settlement was in 1585 on Roanoke Island in modern day Dare County in North Carolina. The colony suffered various troubles, and when a supply ship came to the site of the settlement in 1590, the colonists had disappeared. The fate of the "Lost Colony" remains a mystery to historians, although a good bet is that the members were absorbed into a local tribe of natives. A second attempt to establish a permanent outpost resulted in the founding of Jamestown in 1607. This one struggled, too, but ultimately survived long enough to be called the first permanent English settlement in North America.

The founding of a colony was more than an economic or military adventure. It also was a legal proceeding. Among other things this meant that a charter had to be drafted to delineate the boundaries, purposes, and activities of the colony as well as the relationship between the colony and its parent government. It is interesting and revealing to investigate these charters in order to see what really motivated both the colonists and those who sent them. When we do this, we perceive an amazing and fundamental evolution in the purpose of colonization. In his very detailed examination of the soul of America, *The Christian Life and Character of the Civil Institutions of the United States*, Benjamin F. Morris writes, that the British colonial era in North America "opened a new chapter in the progress of events and in the history of colonizing countries. Hitherto, conquest, ambition, worldly glory, had often marked the settlement of newly discovered territory. God now changes the scene, and, for the first time in the history of the world, the colonization of a new and great continent begins from the purest and profoundest religious convictions and principles." [p. 61] He continued, "The American colonies had a profound conviction of the essential need of religion as the only true basis of civil government." [p. 243] Undoubtedly, this claim seems foreign and farfetched to those who have been brought up imbibing the poisonous elixir served by the educational establishment, but it becomes self-evident once we look at the charters of many of the original British colonies. Let's look at a few.

The 1606 charter for founding a colony in Virginia, which applied to those who established Jamestown, stated that among the purposes of this colony was the "propagating of Christian religion to such people as yet live in darkness." Three years later, in 1609, another charter for this territory stated, "the principal effect which we can desire or expect of this action is the conversion…of the people in those parts unto the true worship of God and Christian religion." Do not miss the fact that the "principal effect" sought in the establishment of the Virginia Colony was essentially the same as Columbus' motivation; namely, to "bring the Word of God to unknown coastlands."

Let's move north a bit to look at the founding of another famous early American settlement: Plymouth Plantation. By the early seventeenth century, many Christians in Britain had become discontent with the Church of England. Some sought to purify it while others determined to separate themselves from it all together

—physically leaving England if necessary. In 1608 a group of these purifiers (Puritans) fled to Amsterdam and then to Leiden, Holland, the following year. After about a decade many of these religious refugees became concerned that they were losing their English heritage—and language—and began to consider another move, this time to the New World. They loaded many of their members and what possessions they could on a ship they had purchased named the Speedwell and departed for Southampton—back in England where they had started. There they loaded a few more people and supplies on the Mayflower, which they had chartered. The two ships departed for America on August 15, 1620, but the Speedwell began taking on so much water that it was feared she could not make the arduous trip across the Atlantic. Both ships returned to England, arriving first at Dartmouth and then at Plymouth. Precious time passed, and the prospect of crossing the angry ocean in winter loomed larger than the sails of the Mayflower. The indigent passengers also had to resort to eating the seed they had packed away for planting their first crop in America. The decision was made for the Mayflower to go it alone before any more time was lost. She departed Plymouth on September 16, 1620.

Sixty-six days later the Mayflower, her crew, and passengers arrived off Cape Cod—well north of the colony of Virginia where they had permission to land. The crew, passengers, and ship were spent after a rough journey that saw the Mayflower crack a main beam which had to be hastily repaired at sea. The decision was made to explore the local area to find a suitable place to settle rather than to continue south to Virginia. The Pilgrims to this new land were exhausted.

In addition to all the challenges of surviving in an unfamiliar wilderness, there was another problem. As mentioned earlier, the founding of a colony was more than an economic or military adventure. It also was a legal proceeding. The colonists had a lawful charter that applied to their intended landing site in Virginia. However, they had no legal document that detailed how they should organize themselves in this new location—so, they created one. It has been called the "Mayflower Compact", and it is the first charter of government written solely in America. That document begins, "In the Name of God, Amen." It then goes on to state that the Pilgrims' journey was "undertaken for the glory of God, and Advancement of the Christian Faith, and the honour of our King and Country…." Once again, it seems that the "principal effect" of the establishment of the Plymouth Plantation was essentially the same as Columbus' motivation: to "bring the Word of God to unknown coastlands."

If there were any doubt regarding this motivation, the 1629 charter for Massachusetts states that "the principal end of this plantation [or colony]" is to "win and incite the natives of…[this] country to the knowledge and obedience of the only true God and Savior of mankind, and the Christian faith…." The words of Benjamin F. Morris cited earlier should be ringing in our ears: "God now changes the scene, and, for the first time in the history of the world, the colonization of a new and great continent begins from the purest and profoundest religious convictions and principles." Oh, but there is more.

The 1632 charter for Maryland proclaimed, "a laudable and pious zeal for extending the Christian religion…." The charter authorizing settlements in North Carolina nearly copied this verbiage by referring to "a laudable and pious zeal for the propagation of the Christian faith…." In 1663 the Rhode Island charter declared the settlers "sober, serious and religious intentions of Godly edifying themselves and one another in the holy Christian faith…." The 1680 Pennsylvania charter cited its "commendable desire to … [convert] the savage natives by gentle and just manners to the love of civil society and Christian religion…."

Before moving on, allow me to boomerang back to the concerns of the habitual complainers who see only the oppression of the native populations in this desire to share Christianity with them. The Quakers established a beautiful, trusting, and loving relationship with most of the natives in their area. The Quakers, who would not fight, were occasionally defended from the attack of some hostile native tribes by the other tribes with whom they had established a relationship of trust. Granted, the relationship between colonists and natives didn't always work that way, but those who demonstrated true Christian values tended to have much better relationships with native populations than those who did not.

The Schools

It wasn't long before the new settlers up and down the Atlantic coast began to turn their attention to the education of their children. As you may suspect after our brief discussion so far, God was at the heart of this endeavor.

Harvard was the first formal institution created for the higher education of the upcoming generations. It was named after John Harvard, a clergyman. Its original motto was "Veritas Christo Et Ecclesiae", which is Latin for "Truth for Christ and the Church." In more secular times that got changed to simply "Veritas" or "Truth." Yale was started by ten Congregationalist clergymen. Its motto was Hebrew for "Christ the Word and Interpreter of the Father, our light and perfection." That, too, has been changed to merely "Light and Truth." Princeton's first year of classes was taught by Reverend Jonathan Dickinson. It's motto was Latin for "Under God she flourishes."

The Revolution

With an educational foundation like this, it should come as no surprise that when the time came to form our own independent government the Founders, like the Pilgrims, would turn to God as their inspiration. But before we could "form our own independent government", we first had to become independent. After decades of bearing the oppressive weight of British despotism—accelerated by a desire to recover the costs of the French and Indian War—the colonials decided they had had enough. It wasn't enough, however, to simply detach. We needed to justify our course of action. We wanted the world and the future to know that we weren't merely a gang of petulant children who didn't like the way the game was going, so we picked up our ball and left the game. We wanted all to know that we were not a crew of greedy farmers and merchants who sought a bigger market share. No, this was a legal and moral dissolution to which we were entitled by nothing less than "the laws of nature and of nature's God." And so we assigned some of our greatest thinkers to the task of writing this "Dissolution Document"; namely, Robert Livingston, Roger Sherman, Benjamin Franklin, John Adams, and Thomas Jefferson. The greatest part of that noble task fell to Jefferson. The declaration they composed mentioned God four times—twice in the beginning and twice in the end. That's how we started it and that's how we ended it.

The first paragraph of the Declaration of Independence argues that we were entitled to a "separate and equal station" among "the Powers of the earth" according to "the Laws of Nature and of Nature's God." The second paragraph proclaims that "all men" "are endowed by their Creator with certain unalienable Rights." This passage will figure prominently in the American philosophy of government that is historically and morally unique and which we will discuss in a later chapter.

In the last paragraph of the Declaration, we proclaimed that we were "appealing to the Supreme Judge of the world for the rectitude of our intentions" in declaring "That these United Colonies are, and of Right ought to be Free and Independent States…." And then we wrapped it all up by announcing our "firm reliance on the Protection of Divine Providence…." The war for independence, which had begun more than a year earlier at the battles of Lexington and Concord on April 19, 1775, was no longer merely a revolt. It was a sacred cause.

The Constitution

The American Revolution officially ended September 3, 1783, with the signing of the Treaty of Paris by John Adams, Benjamin Franklin, and John Jay for the United States. It was formally ratified by the Continental Congress on January 14, 1784. Now it was time for the colonists to put on their big-boy pants and start acting like a united nation. It didn't go well at first. Our original constitution, the Articles of Confederation, proved inadequate to the task of reining in the disparate interests of the various states and leading them into a secure and prosperous future together. This was quickly apparent, and already in 1785 there was serious talk about holding a constitutional gathering to fix the Articles. That meeting finally convened on May 25, 1787, in Philadelphia, Pennsylvania. That assembly also did not start well. Just a month in to the deliberations, serious problems had arisen, especially concerning how both large, populous states and small, sparsely inhabited states could be treated fairly in a national confederation. Some delegates to the Constitutional Convention had stopped attending. The whole thing was about to come unraveled when on June 28, Benjamin Franklin, the senior member of the convention at eighty-one years of age, stood to make a motion.

> "In the beginning of the Contest with G. Britain, when we were sensible of danger, we had daily prayer in this room for Divine protection.—Our prayers, Sir, were heard, & they were graciously answered…I have lived, Sir, a long time, and the longer I live, the more convincing proofs I see of this truth—that God Governs in the affairs of men. And if a sparrow cannot fall to the ground without His notice, is it probable that an empire can rise without His aid? We have been assured, Sir, in

the Sacred Writings, that 'except the Lord build the House, they labor in vain that build it.' I firmly believe this; and I also believe that without his concurring aid we shall succeed in this political building no better than the Builders of Babel...I therefore beg leave to move—that henceforth prayers imploring the assistance of Heaven, and its blessings on our deliberations, be held in this Assembly every morning before we proceed to business, and that one or more of the clergy of this city be requested to officiate in that service."

Franklin's motion was seconded, discussed, and voted down. It was not disapproved because the members objected to prayer. It was voted down because the Convention had no money to pay a member of the clergy to come pray for it. (Ah, for the good old days when our representatives sought to live within their budgets.) The Convention did recess for three days. During that time many members prayed and engaged in other Christianly fellowship. As Jonathan Dayton (a delegate from New Jersey and, at 27, the youngest delegate) noted, "We assembled again...every unfriendly feeling had been expelled, and a spirit of conciliation had been cultivated." During the next two-and-a-half months, the delegates proceeded to draft one of the most remarkable political documents of history.

Before proceeding, let us pause to remember something Benjamin F. Morris wrote, as quoted earlier. "The American colonies had a profound conviction of the essential need of religion as the only true basis of civil government." That same "essential need" was acknowledged and indulged by the Framers of the Constitution. Indeed, it would have been difficult for them to ignore that essential need. They were immersed in an intellectual and cultural milieu that recognized it. Before looking at some of the specific influences of the Bible manifested in the Constitution, let's peruse the thoughts of some who encapsulated and advocated the popular sentiment of the day.

John Adams, first vice-president and second president of the United States, wrote, "religion and virtue are the only foundations...of republicanism and of all free governments." He also wrote, "Our Constitution was made only for a moral and religious people. It is wholly inadequate to the government of any other." Before proceeding, note Adams' use of the word "foundation." You will see that many others believed morals and religion to be an essential base for the establishment of free governments.

Patrick Henry, a politician who twice served as governor of Virginia and orator who gave us the famous words "give me liberty, or give me death!", wrote, "The great pillars of all government and social life ... [are] virtue, morality, and religion" and "It cannot be emphasized too clearly and too often that this nation was founded, not by religionists, but by Christians; not on religion, but on the gospel of Jesus Christ."

Charles Carroll, Signer of the Declaration of Independence, wrote, "without morals a republic cannot subsist any length of time; they therefore who are decrying the Christian religion, whose morality is so sublime and pure...are undermining the solid foundation of morals, the best security for the duration of free governments."

Noah Webster, lexicographer and educator, wrote, "the moral principle and precepts contained in the Scriptures ought to form the basis of all our civil constitutions and laws" and "the Christian religion, in its purity, is the basis, or rather the source of all genuine freedom in government ... and I am persuaded that no civil government of a republican form can exist and be durable in which the principles of that religion have not a controlling influence."

John, Jay, diplomat and first Chief Justice of the U.S. Supreme Court, wrote, it is "the duty of all wise, free, and virtuous governments to countenance and encourage virtue and religion" and "The Bible is the best of all books, for it is the word of God and teaches us the way to be happy in this world and in the next. Continue therefore to read it and to regulate your life by its precepts."

William Paterson, signer of the Constitution and U.S. Supreme Court Justice, wrote, "Religion and morality ... [are] necessary to good government, good order, and good laws."

Joseph Story, founder of the Harvard School of Law and U.S. Supreme Court Justice, wrote, "One of the beautiful boasts of our municipal jurisprudence is that Christianity is a part of the Common Law.... There never has been a period in which the Common Law did not recognize Christianity as lying at its foundations.... I verily believe Christianity necessary to the support of civil society."

The Biblical influence on the drafters of the Constitution is clearly evident in the document they composed. Let's look at just a few examples. As stated in the opening paragraph, or Preamble, of the Constitution, the purpose of the document is "to form a more perfect Union, establish justice, insure domestic tranquility, provide for the common defense, promote the general welfare, and secure the blessings of liberty to ourselves and our posterity…." In order to accomplish these objectives, the people, through accepting this document, "do ordain and establish this Constitution for the United States of America." Whoa. Wait a minute. Isn't "ordain" a religious word? Sometimes. It can mean merely "establish", but the authors said "establish" just two words after "ordain." It is highly unlikely that a bunch of obsessive word-smiths would intend "ordain" to be repeated needlessly. And once we exclude "establish" as the intended meaning of "ordain', then, yes, we are left with only religious definitions; like, "to invest with a ministerial function or sacerdotal power" found in Noah Webster's first dictionary, *The American Dictionary of the English Language*, published in 1828. Webster was a contemporary of the Founders and Framers, so they would have had a common understanding to the words they used.

So, the Constitution was consecrated to do the work of God. More than that, it required that the work of the Constitution be done in a Godly manner. Article 1 of the Constitution details the legislative process. Article I, Section 7, of the Constitution describes how laws are made. Once both houses of Congress (the House of Representatives and the Senate) pass the same bill, that bill is forwarded to the president for his signature. The president may veto a bill, but he only has a limited amount of time to act. The Constitution says, "If any bill shall not be returned by the President within ten days (Sundays excepted) after it shall have been presented to him, the same shall be a law in like manner as if he had signed it…." In other words, the president has ten days to act, not counting Sundays. Why are Sundays excluded? Obviously, because that is the Christian sabbath day, and you are not supposed to toil on the sabbath even if you are the President of the United States. Here is an example of the "Blue Laws" written into the Constitution.

The Constitution is admired and praised for many things. One of these is its division of power into three branches of government: the judicial, the legislative, and the executive. Did this come about as an act of original genius by the Framers? No. Actually, they were recognizing the genius of an Other. The Old Testament prophet, Isaiah, wrote the text of the Biblical book that bears his name about 700 years before Christ. In the twenty-second verse of the thirty-third chapter of that book, Isaiah points to the three aspects of governing power. "For the Lord is our judge, the Lord is our lawgiver, the Lord is our king; he will save us." God is our judge (judicial), our lawgiver (legislative), and our king (executive). It's a good thing the Founders and Framers were, almost to a man, devout Christians. If not, the document they composed would not have been nearly so noble.

There are many other Biblical principles embedded in the Constitution, but let's jump to the very end. Right after Article VII and right before the signatures comes these words: "DONE in convention by the unanimous consent of the States present the seventeenth day of September in the Year of our Lord one thousand seven hundred and eighty seven, and of the independence of the United States of America the twelfth." Gee, who do you suppose this "Lord" of ours is who lived one thousand, seven hundred and eighty-seven years earlier? Obviously, it is Jesus, the Christ. Now, some may try to dismiss this as merely a literary practice sometimes even indulged in by atheist. Not likely. You see, there is another date mentioned in the Constitution, 1808, which deals with the slave trade. It simply refers to "the Year one thousand eight hundred and eight." No "Year of our Lord" here. So, it surely looks like the use of this phrase was a deliberate flourish and nod to Christianity by the Framers.

All this argues that the Constitution of the United States is "ordained" by the people to do the work of God; it recognizes uniquely Christian and Biblical practices; and it proclaims Jesus Christ to be our "Lord." As we prepare to wrap up this chapter on American Genesis, let's first look at a few actions taken by our first Congress and our first President.

The Government

The founding of the United States of America was a watershed event in history. Nothing like this had ever happened before. Those who were granted the honor to initiate the first government under the Constitution back in 1789 were impressed with the great opportunity they had been given and with the grave responsibility that had been placed upon them. They had to get it right. Both their academic training and their personal experience convinced them that this meant turning to and yielding to God. This tradition had been honored throughout the Revolution. National days of thanksgiving and of "humiliation, fasting, and prayer" were proclaimed by the Continental Congress at least twice a year during the war. With their vision focused heavenward and their spirits obedient to God, they began their work. Along with Noah Webster they firmly believed that "the moral principle and precepts contained in the Scriptures ought to form the basis of all our civil constitutions and laws."

One of the very first tasks undertaken by the very first Congress was to select a chaplain for each house. William Linn was selected for the House of Representatives and Samuel Provost was chosen for the Senate. Don't miss the significance of this. Congress voted to hire a Christian pastor to pray at government functions and to be paid with public funds. Apparently, the very people who wrote the First Amendment didn't understand the principle of separation of church and state as well as do many of our modern pundits. And speaking of the First Amendment and the other nine which comprised the Bill of Rights....

Once the work of the Constitutional Congress ended on September 17, 1787, the work of ratifying that document among the states began. A few problems arose, however. For example, many people felt the Constitution did not do enough to protect the very rights we had fought to establish during the eight-and-a-half years of the Revolution. They wanted to specifically enumerate many of our most fundamental rights, which the Constitution did not do. And so a compromise was worked out; namely, vote to ratify the Constitution and we promise to draft a bill of rights during the first Congress that will be amended to the Constitution. That promise was honored. After months of proposing and debating and writing and rewriting, the Bill of Rights was approved on September 25, 1789. Very shortly afterward, on the same day, Representative Elias Boudinot from New Jersey introduced a Thanksgiving resolution in the House calling for "a day of public thanksgiving and prayer to be observed by acknowledging, with grateful hearts, the many signal favors of Almighty God, especially by affording them an opportunity peaceably to establish a Constitution of government for their safety and happiness." The people who composed and approved the First Amendment had no problem officially proposing a day to thank God for what they believed He

—not they—had done. The measure passed the House and, three days later, passed the Senate. It was then forwarded to President George Washington. Would this pose a problem? He had been the president of the Constitutional Convention. Would he take any offense at declaring a public demonstration of thanks to God. See for yourself. On October 3, 1789, Washington signed the Thanksgiving proclamation which contained these words: "Whereas it is the duty of all Nations to acknowledge the providence of Almighty God, to obey his will, to be grateful for his benefits, and humbly to implore his protection and favor...I do recommend and assign Thursday the 26th day of November next to be devoted by the People of these States to the service of that great and glorious Being, who is the beneficent Author of all the good that was, that is, or that will be." The resolute commander of the Continental Army had now assumed the role of resolute preacher to the nation. That is what leaders do. They shepherd the people along those pathways that are in their best interests.

Speaking of George Washington, how did he initiate the office of President under the Constitution?

Thursday, April 30, 1789, New York City. Beginning at 9:00 a.m., church bells throughout the city began to ring. The divine chorus continued for thirty minutes. Three-and-a-half hours later, a military contingent arrived at Franklin House to escort the president-elect to Federal Hall. The procession took thirty minutes. The members of both houses of Congress were notified of the president-elect's arrival. At 2:00 p.m., the oath of office was administered on the balcony of the Senate chambers overlooking Broad Street. The president placed his hand on a Bible and took the oath as prescribed in the Constitution. He then added four more words, "So help me God", and bent over to kiss the Bible. The president, humbled by the event, seemed uneasy and presented his inaugural address in a quiet voice, maintaining a subdued and respectful demeanor. Upon conclusion of the formal ceremonies, the inaugural party proceeded to Saint Paul's Chapel for a worship service that included singing the hymn, *Te Deum*. Its opening words, "Te Deum laudamus," can be translated "Thee, O God, we praise." That evening the President had his dinner alone.

In his inaugural address, Washington sounded more like a Biblical prophet than a secular politician. He hastened to express his gratitude to God and to ensure that all who would hear his words would understand their obligation to do likewise. He affirmed that, "it would be peculiarly improper to omit in this first official act my fervent supplications to that Almighty Being who rules over the universe, who presides in the councils of nations, and whose providential aids can supply every human defect, that His benediction may consecrate to the liberties and happiness of the people of the United States a Government instituted by themselves for these essential purposes, and may enable every instrument employed in its administration to execute with success the functions allotted to his charge." He then looked back at the recent history in which he had played so prominent a role and saw the superintending hand of God hovering over the entire process. "No people can be bound to acknowledge and adore the Invisible Hand which conducts the affairs of men more than those of the United States. Every step by which they have advanced to the character of an independent nation seems to have been distinguished by some token of providential agency...." Then, ominously, he prophesied, "we ought to be no less persuaded that the propitious smiles of Heaven can never be expected on a nation that disregards the eternal rules of order and right which Heaven itself has ordained...."

Few people had seen more clearly than George Washington the role that God can and will play in the affairs of humankind. The essential lessons he learned from his own personal experience boils down to these: God got us here. God will only keep us here as long as we obey Him. There is a quote that has been attributed to Washington, but which has been dismissed as likely spurious; namely, ""It is impossible to rightly govern a nation without God and the Bible." It may be spurious in the sense that Washington may not have said those words, but his other words confirm that this was his firm conviction. To bolster that claim, consider once again the words just quoted from his first inaugural address in light of the words quoted earlier from his first Thanksgiving proclamation; namely, "it is the duty of all Nations to acknowledge the providence of Almighty God, to obey his will, to be grateful for his benefits, and humbly to implore his protection and favor...." It surely sounds like he is saying that it is impossible to rightly govern a nation without God and the Bible.

Te Deum Laudamus

To quickly summarize this chapter on the American Genesis, we have seen that the discoverer of this continent, the colonists, the people who established their colleges, the Founders, the Framers, the Declaration of Independence, the Constitution, our first president, the first Congress and many other luminaries of our founding saw their paramount responsibility to be the service of God. They made Him the center of everything they did. He was the foundation of everything they built. God is woven into our national DNA. America without God simply is not America.

Discussion

"If you know how a tree starts, you will not only know what kind of fruit it will bear, you also will know how to nurture that tree so it will bear much fruit. The same applies to nations." Do you think that knowing more about the origins of the United States is important for preserving our character as a nation? Why or why not?

"Our formal educational system—exemplified in our network of public, government run schools—has lied to us for decades. It has had reason to do so, and that reason has nothing to do with what is best for America and its people." Do you think this is true? If so, what is the reason for lying to the people? Who is behind encouraging this lie?

Were you surprised to learn that Columbus' purpose *"in seeking 'undiscovered worlds' was to, 'bring the Gospel of Jesus Christ to the heathens' and to 'bring the Word of God to unknown coastlands'"*? Why do you suppose this important fact is excluded from most modern textbooks and curricula?

In his book, *The Christian Life and Character of the Civil Institutions of the United States*, Benjamin F. Morris writes, that the British colonial era in North America *"opened a new chapter in the progress of events and in the history of colonizing countries. Hitherto, conquest, ambition, worldly glory, had often marked the settlement of newly discovered territory. God now changes the scene, and, for the first time in the history of the world, the colonization of a new and great continent begins from the purest and profoundest religious convictions and principles."* This seems to be verified by the charters of many colonies which included objectives like *"propagating of Christian religion to such people as yet live in darkness"* or words to that same effect. Have you ever heard this before? Why aren't the public schools teaching this?

Benjamin F. Morris also wrote, *"The American colonies had a profound conviction of the essential need of religion as the only true basis of civil government."* Why is religion so important to the success of civil government? If civil government is not founded upon religion, what would be the foundation? Do you think any religion could successfully create a solid foundation for civil government? Christianity was the religion of the Founders and Framers, so that is the religion they used to form the basis of our civil government. Do you think Christianity would do a better or worse job than other religions at providing a basis for civil government? Why?

Some of the colonial charters expressed an intention to *"win and incite the natives of...[this] country to the knowledge and obedience of the only true God and Savior of mankind, and the Christian faith...."* Do you see this as an offense against the native population's right to religious liberty or as a spiritual blessing intended to uplift these people? Would your answer change depending on how the colonists attempted to *"win and incite the natives of...[this] country to the knowledge and obedience of the only true God and Savior of mankind, and the Christian faith...."*?

The mottos of our earliest educational institutions included references to God. In more recent times these mottos have been changed and have excluded any reference to God. What does this tell you?

The author writes that by the time the Declaration of Independence was written, the revolution *"was no longer merely a revolt. It was a sacred cause."* What evidence is there to support this claim?

During the Constitutional Convention in 1787, Benjamin Franklin said, *"that God Governs in the affairs of men. And if a sparrow cannot fall to the ground without His notice, is it probable that an empire can rise without His aid?"* Do you agree that God governs in the affairs of men—or, at least, that He should? Do you agree that it is improbable for an empire to rise without His aid? There have been many pagan empires that have arisen over the course of human history. Is this proof that Franklin was wrong, or that God is at work among pagan people as well?

John Adams wrote, *"Our Constitution was made only for a moral and religious people. It is wholly inadequate to the government of any other."* Adams is saying that our Constitution will not work unless the population is moral and religious. Why would this be true? (This will be discussed in a later chapter.) If Adams is right, what happens if we cease to be a moral and religious people?

The author claims *"the Constitution of the United States is "ordained" by the people to do the work of God; it recognizes uniquely Christian and Biblical practices; and it proclaims Jesus Christ to be our 'Lord.'"* Does the evidence back this claim? If so, then how valid is the concept of "separation of church and state" as it is currently understood?

The same people who wrote the First Amendment also used public funds to hire Christian pastors (the chaplains for each of the houses of the legislature) to pray at government events in public buildings. That would not pass muster today given our understanding of the principle of "separation of church and state." So, did the authors of the First Amendment not understand what they had written, or are modern interpreters at fault?

In his first Thanksgiving Proclamation, President Washington wrote, *"it is the duty of all Nations to acknowledge the providence of Almighty God, to obey his will, to be grateful for his benefits, and humbly to implore his protection and favor...."* Can you imagine a modern-day president saying the same thing? If not, why not? So, who is wrong—Washington for honoring God or modern politicians for ignoring Him?

The author concludes this chapter by saying, *"America without God simply is not America."* Do you agree? What will America be like without God?

CHAPTER FIVE:

George Washington—The

Indispensable Man

The chronicles of secular history record many instances where the influence of a single individual fundamentally changed everything that followed—whether for good or ill. Alexander the Great, Aristotle, Julius Caesar, Charlemagne, Martin Luther, Queen Elizabeth I, Queen Victoria, Isaac Newton, Charles Darwin, Karl Marx, Vladimir Lenin, Adolf Hitler, Mao Zedong.

The chronicles of Biblical history document the same phenomenon. Adam, Eve, Abraham, Sarah, Jacob, Moses, Joshua, David, Solomon, Ahab, Jezebel, Jesus, Paul.

There is another name that must be included in the first list; and, although not Biblical, we have to wonder if this name should also be included among the greatest of God's human agents: George Washington. A biography written by James Thomas Flexner describes him appropriately: the Indispensable Man. Had everything else been present among the eighteenth century American colonials except George Washington, would the Revolution have been won? If the Constitutional Convention had gathered without Washington as its presiding officer, would it have been so brilliantly crafted? If the first Constitutional government had assembled in 1789 without Washington as its president, would that government have survived and ushered the advent of history's grandest, most powerful, wealthiest, and noblest nation? We can never know the answer to such hypotheticals, but the fact that we can even ponder the possibilities detailed above testifies to the overwhelming influence of George Washington. No consideration of America's essential nature and manifest destiny can exclude him; and so we will briefly highlight a few revealing aspects of his history as it affects our heritage.

To set the stage, let us first look at a few biographical tidbits in order to establish the context for what is to follow. Washington was born February 22, 1732, at Pope's Creek, in the Virginia Colony. He was trained to be a surveyor, and he worked at that trade from 1747 to 1752. From an early age he had an interest in military matters and wanted to join the British Royal Navy. Although family members talked him out of that career, he joined the Virginia Regiment in 1753 and later became the commander of all of Virginia's colonial forces. He served as an aid to British General Edward Braddock during the French and Indian War. He loved agriculture and lived as a farmer with vast land holdings in Virginia and elsewhere. His political career began at an early age, and he served in the Virginia House of Burgesses from 1758 to 1776. He married Martha Dandridge Custis in 1759, which significantly enlarged his land holdings and wealth. Washington served as the only commander of the Continental Army from 1775 to 1783. He presided over the Constitutional Convention in 1787, and was unanimously elected President of the United States by the Electoral College twice, serving from 1789 to 1797. He died December 14, 1799.

The event that first boosted Washington into prominence was his conduct during the French and Indian War, which was fought from 1754 until 1763. It was the American theater of the European Seven Year's War. The colonial interests of the British and French began to collide as the French, based in what today is eastern Canada, sought to expand westward and southward and the British moved deeper and deeper into the North American Continent.

In 1753 Major Washington was sent to the vicinity of modern-day Erie, Pennsylvania, as an ambassador of the British crown to meet with French officials and some of their Indian allies. In 1754 he was sent with some troops to assist the construction of a fort at present-day Pittsburgh. Before arriving there, he ambushed a French scouting party resulting in the death of the leader of the French detachment. The French responded by attacking Washington's meager forces holed up in the hastily constructed defenses erected by Washington known as Fort Necessity. Overwhelmed and cut off, Washington surrendered. He and his men were released on parole, curiously enough on July 4, 1754, and returned to Virginia. This is often marked as the beginning of the French and Indian War.

The following year, 1755, Washington served as a volunteer aid to British General Edward Braddock. Washington had studied the fighting techniques and tactics of the native populations and advised Braddock to emulate them. Braddock refused—a decision that would cost him dearly. In the spring of 1755, the British began a campaign to attack French fortifications in North America. Braddock, the commander of all British forces in America, personally led the intended attack on Fort Duquesne in the vicinity of modern Pittsburgh. On July 9, after crossing the Monongahela River, the British forces were attacked by the French and their native allies using the same tactics Washington had recommended to Braddock. It was a rout. The British suffered 977 casualties out of the 1,400 troops and officers engaged. Every officer—except Washington—was killed or wounded. That night, Washington found four bullet holes in his jacket, but he had not been touched. The French and Indians suffered only 39 casualties among their force of about 900. Braddock was wounded and would die July 13. Washington took over the evacuation of the remaining forces and later was hailed as the "Hero of the Monongahela." Washington remained in the Virginia militia and participated in the ultimate capture of Fort Duquesne in 1758. He rose to the rank of colonel and commander of the Virginia Regiment, but was refused a commission in the British Army and resigned from the provincial militia.

Washington's survival in the Battle of the Monongahela was remarkable—some would argue miraculous. One observer of the battle wrote, "I expected every moment to see him fall. Nothing but the superintending care of Providence could have saved him." Washington agreed writing, "By the all-powerful dispensations of Providence, I have been protected beyond all human probability or expectation." Another observer weighed in with an observation that is not only revealing, it is otherworldly.

Colonial veterans of the French and Indian War were given land grants by the British. In the fall of 1770, Washington and several others traveled to the Ohio territory to examine the land that had been granted to Washington. During that trip, the Washington party was confronted by a group of natives including an elderly and greatly respected sachem, or chief, especially of multiple tribes. Washington invited them to share dinner. The sachem remained quiet and withdrawn until after the meal when he rose to speak through an interpreter. This is part of the tale that Washington's friend, Dr. James Craik, recorded.

"I am a chief, and the ruler over many tribes. My influence extends to the waters of the great lakes, and to the far blue mountains. I have traveled a long and weary path that I might see the young warrior of the great battle.

"It was on the day when the white man's blood mixed with the streams of our forests that I first beheld this chief. I called to my young men and said, Mark yon tall and daring warrior? He is not of the red-coat tribe—he hath an Indian's wisdom, and his warriors fight as we do—himself is alone exposed. Quick, let your aim be certain, and he dies. Our rifles were leveled, rifles which but for him knew not how to miss—'twas all in vain; a power mightier far than we shielded him from harm. He cannot die in battle.

"I am old, and soon shall be gathered to the great council fire of my fathers in the land of shades; but ere I go there is something bids me speak in the voice of prophecy. Listen! The Great Spirit protects that man, and guides his destinies—he will become the chief of nations, and a people yet unborn will hail him as the founder of a mighty empire."

Years later, during the Revolutionary War, Dr. Craik was approached by several of Washington's senior officers. The next day Washington's army would attack the British as they left Philadelphia on their way back to New York. It would be recorded as the Battle of Monmouth Courthouse, June 28, 1778. They pleaded with Craik to tell their commander-in-chief to be more reserved in the conduct of the battle and stay out of the fray where he could be wounded or killed. As was established in the French and Indian War, Washington had a reputation for inspirational courage and being up front in the thick of the fighting where his life was in grave danger. He was too valuable to risk losing. Even back then he was recognized to be the "indispensable man." The senior officers knew Washington would not listen to them, but hoped maybe he could be influenced by his old friend. Craik said he would pass along their request, but added that, although Washington would appreciate their concern, it wouldn't change anything. Washington had to be Washington. Then Craik relayed the story of the old Indian prophecy. "He cannot die in battle…The Great Spirit protects that man, and guides his destinies…." The officers left the meeting shaking their heads, dismissing the foolishness of the old Indian's superstitions.

Sure enough, during the next day's battle, Washington was front and center leading his troops. A British cannonball hit a few feet from Washington mounted on his horse. It splattered him with mud, but he was unfazed. He wiped the mud off his face and continued barking out orders. One of the officers at the meeting the night before witnessed the event. He looked at Craik, who also was nearby, and gestured as though to say "I told you so!" Craik merely smiled and pointed upward to Heaven as if to say, "No, I told you so. A Great Spirit protects that man. He cannot die in battle."

It was not the only time Washington and his troops benefitted from what can only be described as weirdly impossible—or miraculous.

Washington was commissioned commander of the Continental Army on June 19, 1775, by the Continental Congress. He traveled northward to Massachusetts and assumed command of the American forces in Cambridge on July 3, 1775. The mass of the British land and sea forces were concentrated in Massachusetts because it had been an early hotbed of the colonial rebellion. Washington quickly moved to surround and contain the British in Boston Harbor. It was a bold move that gave the colonials the high ground overlooking the harbor, but Washington lacked the firepower to exploit his advantage. During the winter of 1775-1776, however, Colonel Henry Knox supervised the transport of more than sixty tons of military supplies captured by the colonials at Fort Ticonderoga which had been held by the British. It was a stunning engineering feat moving those supplies, including more than 50 cannons, across mountains and rivers to deliver them to Washington's troops at Boston. Beginning March 2, the American forces, using their recently-arrived artillery, began a two-day bombardment of the British below them in the harbor. On the night of March 4, Washington moved several thousand of his troops along with some Ticonderoga cannons into positions on the Dorchester Heights. British General William Howe, realizing the desperation of his situation, ordered an evacuation of Boston after eight years of British occupation. It was a staggering defeat for the British and an extraordinary (miraculous?) victory for Washington and his army—and he knew it. Regarding that event, Washington wrote to the General Assembly of Massachusetts, "It must be ascribed to the interposition of that Providence which has manifestly appeared in our behalf through the whole of this important struggle."

But the "whole of this important struggle" had just begun. The British had left Boston, not America. They had surrendered the field, not the war. Now the question was, where would they strike next? Washington correctly divined that it would be New York City, so he hastened to move his army more than two hundred miles south to be there when they arrived.

In early July, 1776, 400 ships delivered 32,000 well-rested British troops under the command of General William Howe. He offered a pardon to the 19,000 rebels under Washington's command. Washington replied, "Those who have committed no fault want no pardon."

On the evening of August 26, Howe maneuvered his troops to attack the Americans. The colonials were no match for the British and were beaten back across the length of Long Island. By the evening of August 29, the surrounded Americans were in desperate trouble. Their backs pressed hard against the East River, they clung to a small plot of land awaiting the next surge by the British, which likely would end the revolution. Washington ordered a nighttime evacuation across the East River from Brooklyn to Manhattan. He went to great lengths to keep his foe in the dark about what he was doing. As would be the case at Dunkirk hundreds of years later, everything that floated was seized to assist the evacuation. Absolute silence was mandated—even horses' hooves were swaddled. If the British learned what Washington was doing, they would immediately attack the divided and vulnerable American army. The evacuation was far from completed when Washington noticed the sky in the east beginning to lighten. This was the worst of all possible events. Half of Washington's meager army was still within striking distance of the superior British forces while the other half was across the river where they could render no assistance. It looked as though the sun would rise on August 30 and on the end of the American rebellion.

But then, moments before the British would be able to see what their enemy was about, a thick, blinding fog arose from the land and sea and covered the continuing evacuation of the Americans. It was recorded that Washington, himself, boarded the last barge across the river, and when he had not yet reached the other side, the fog lifted. If only General Howe and his British masters had known of the "Old Indian Prophesy"—the Great Spirit protects that man, and guides his destinies—the war could have ended much sooner and with many fewer casualties. They did not, and the war continued.

Washington and his army conducted a fighting delay in the months to come staying just out of reach of the British. By December, 1776, however, many patriots were disheartened. Their enlistments would be up in a matter of weeks. The Patriots needed a reason to believe that their cause could still prevail. General Washington gave them one. Trenton.

On Christmas night, Washington led an audacious and unexpected attack on the Hessian barracks in Trenton, New Jersey. The Hessians were German mercenaries whom the British hired to augment their own forces and to minimize casualties from among the sons of British families. The Hessians were very proficient and savage.

After crossing the Delaware River, Washington rode up and down the nearly mile long column of troops urging them to continue despite the horrible winter weather. Shortly after 8 o'clock on the morning of December 26, three columns formed to begin their assault upon the expert and vicious Hessians. Washington led the middle column. Three Hessian regiments quickly formed to repulse the attackers. The Hessian commander, Colonel Johann Rall, ordered repeated counterattacks which Washington skillfully repulsed. Rall was mortally wounded, and many of his veteran troops fled in the face of the withering Patriot attack. In only one hour of fighting, the Continental army captured nearly 900 Hessian soldiers and officers along with a large supply of muskets, bayonets, swords, and cannons. Less than two weeks later, on January 3, 1777, Washington's soldiers attacked and defeated British forces near Princeton, New Jersey. The Patriot cause had reason to continue the fight. And they did.

After years of indecisive fighting among the mid and northern Atlantic colonies, the British decided to bring the war to the southern colonies, hoping to discourage them and cut off their support for the rest of the Patriot army. British commander, Lord Cornwallis, had been instrumental in conducting this campaign in the south. Cornwallis was a brilliant commander, but in an uncharacteristic blunder, he led his forces between the York and James Rivers, leaving him little room to maneuver. He had counted on the support of the British Navy operating in the Chesapeake Bay to cover his movement. Washington, finally enjoying the support of both the French Army and Navy, marched his army south from the outskirts of New York City. The French Navy cut off Cornwallis from support by the British Navy and trapped the British ground forces in the village of Yorktown. Washington and his French ally, General Rochambeau, closed in on their prey. The battle began October 9, 1781. Washington commenced a merciless bombardment with his artillery while maneuvering his infantry closer and closer to Cornwallis' defenses. Upon the capture of Redoubts 9 and 10, on the night of October 14, the British situation became hopeless. The Patriots used these reinforced, elevated earthworks to position their own cannons and pounded the remaining British forces in the town. During the course of the battle, the British suffered 8,589 casualties while the Americans registered a mere 389. Cornwallis surrendered October 19, 1781. Although the war would not officially end for nearly another two years, Yorktown was the last major battle. The impossible had happened. Or, maybe not. When the Great Spirit protects and guides destinies, nothing is impossible, as George Washington knew very well.

Washington would preside over the drafting of the Constitution and would be elected first President of the United States—the only person to be unanimously elected by the Electoral College, twice. The incalculable value of this indispensable man cannot be overstated; but there still are two other matters that require our attention: the claim that he was a deist and the fact that he was a slaveowner.

* * *

Washington and Deism

I suspect that among those who think they know George Washington's religious affiliation, most would state that he was a deist. This notion was popularized by historian Paul Boller in his biography, *George Washington and Religion*, printed on the two hundredth anniversary of Washington's birth. The claim of Washington's Deism is shattered in Peter Lilllback's thousand-page tome, *George Washington's Sacred* Fire. Let's briefly consider the evidence.

First of all, "Deism" is a term used chiefly to describe an intellectual movement of the 17th and 18th centuries that accepted the existence of a creator on the basis of reason but rejected the belief in a supernatural deity who interacts with humankind. The god of the Deists was not a personal one. He was likened to a divine watchmaker who designed the watch, built it, wound it, then let it run down without any further interference. Accordingly, there was no point in worshipping, praying, or going to church. The Deist God probably wasn't listening, and even if he were, he wouldn't intervene. George Washington did all three of the above; and, as we have seen, he credited God with intervening in human affairs.

Washington attended and donated to churches where the leaders had to affirm their belief in the key doctrines of the Christian faith. He paid for pews at both his local Pohick Church and Christ Church in Alexandria. His pastor, Lee Massey, wrote, "I never knew so constant an attendant in church as Washington." "Although he never once used the word 'Deist' in his voluminous writings, he often mentioned religion, Christianity, and the Gospel. He spoke of Christ as 'the divine Author of our blessed religion.' He encouraged missionaries who were seeking to 'Christianize' the 'aboriginals.' He took an oath in a private letter, 'on my honor and the faith of a Christian.' "He wrote of 'the blessed religion revealed in the Word of God.' He encouraged seekers to learn 'the religion of Jesus Christ.' He even told his soldiers, 'To the distinguished Character of Patriot, it should be our highest Glory to add the more distinguished Character of Christian.'" [*George Washington's Sacred Fire*, Peter Lillback]

As already noted, in Washington's first inaugural address he witnessed that "Every step, by which they [the colonies] have advanced to the character of an independent nation, seems to have been distinguished by some token of providential agency..." He also predicted "we ought to be no less persuaded that the propitious smiles of Heaven, can never be expected on a nation that disregards the eternal rules of order and right, which Heaven itself has ordained...." These are not things a Deist would believe. Nor would a Deist ever state, as Washington did in his first Thanksgiving Proclamation, that "it is the duty of all Nations to acknowledge the providence of Almighty God, to obey his will, to be grateful for his benefits, and humbly to implore his protection and favor..."

The inescapable verdict which this and a wealth of other information demand is this: George Washington was a Christian, and like virtually all the other Founders and Framers, he believed that Christianity was the foundation of our republic.

* * *

Washington and Slavery

How do we reconcile the record of George Washington as a great liberator—a warrior for liberty and rights—with the fact that he owned slaves? Some have sought to impugn the reputation of Washington because of this apparent hypocrisy. A fair and accurate accounting tells a different tale.

Washington was born into a slave society, so he was raised thinking this was the normal state of affairs. To his credit, he came to detest the practice, but ending it wasn't as simple as merely freeing one's slaves. Freed slaves in the South were often recaptured and sold back into slavery, often to abusive owners. Accordingly, it often would be preferable for a slave to remain with a benevolent master than risk being emancipated only to end up recaptured and sold to an abusive overlord. What was needed was a statewide legislative solution to the matter—something Washington sought. In a letter to Robert Morris dated April 12, 1786, Washington wrote, "There is not a man living who wishes more sincerely than I do to see a plan adopted for the abolition of slavery; but there is only one proper and effectual mode by which it can be accomplished, and that is by legislative authority; and this, so far as my suffrages will go, shall not be wanting." In another letter to John Sinclair, Washington showed that he had been studying the matter and searching for a solution. He wrote, "There are in Pennsylvania laws for the gradual abolition of slavery, which neither Virginia nor Maryland have at present, but which nothing is more certain than that they must have, and at a period not remote."

These letters and other public pronouncements show Washington's heart and mind were in the right place regarding slavery. But did his actions follow his feelings and beliefs? Yes. Washington treated his slaves humanely. Slave children were taught to read and write. This was a rare practice among slave owners because the ability to read and write improved a slave's chances of living independently of his masters—something the masters did not want to encourage. The debts of many Washington slaves were forgiven. He paid to advertise in British newspapers encouraging settlers to come to America where Washington would provide land and "day-laborers." The "day-laborers" would be slaves whom Washington could safely emancipate because they had a connection with a job and piece of land. This substantially reduced the likelihood of being captured and sold back into slavery. All his slaves were emancipated shortly after his death. George provided an annual pension to his freed slaves, including William Lee, his personal valet. Richard Allen, a former slave, and founder of the African Methodist Episcopal (AME) Church eulogized Washington saying, "He has watched over us, and viewed our degraded and afflicted state with compassion and pity—his heart was not insensible to our sufferings."

It is not hard to make the case that George Washington is the greatest American. At a minimum, he must be included on a very short list for that honor. It also is not hard to see the hand of God guiding and protecting him. "The Great Spirit protects that man, and guides his destinies—he will become the chief of nations, and a people yet unborn will hail him as the founder of a mighty empire." He deserves our utmost honor and respect; and modern Americans would be well-advised to emulate his beliefs, his integrity, and his commitment to his beloved homeland.

Discussion

Imagine George Washington had never existed. Would the United States exist? Argue your case.

The author writes, *"we have to wonder if this name [George Washington] should also be included among the greatest of God's human agents...."* Do you wonder? What case can be made to support this claim?

If you had heard the Old Indian Prophesy at the beginning of the American Revolution, would you have believed it? If you had heard the Old Indian Prophesy at the end of the American Revolution, would you have believed it?

"The incalculable value of this indispensable man cannot be overstated...." Do you agree, or do you think the author is indulging in hyperbole?

In a general order issued by Washington shortly before the Battle of Monmouth Courthouse, Washington wrote, *"To the distinguished Character of Patriot, it should be our highest Glory to add the more distinguished Character of Christian."* Washington thought it was more "distinguished" to be a Christian than a patriot. Do you? Why?

In his first Inaugural Address, President Washington said, "the propitious smiles of Heaven, can never be expected on a nation that disregards the eternal rules of order and right, which Heaven itself has ordained...." Do you agree? If so, what do you think happens to a nation that stops following God?

George Washington owned slaves which were never freed until after his death. Is that all that needs to be said on the subject? Should Washington's reputation as a freedom fighter be discarded and his statues brought down for this reason alone; or are there extenuating circumstances? What are those extenuating circumstances?

The author concludes the chapter on the indispensable man by claiming, *"It is not hard to make the case that George Washington is the greatest American. At a minimum, he must be included on a very short list for that honor."* Whom else would you recommend for that list? Why?

"He deserves our utmost honor and respect; and modern Americans would be well-advised to emulate his beliefs, his integrity, and his commitment to his beloved homeland." Do you think Washington is worth emulating, or do you think this is corny and old-fashioned?

CHAPTER SIX:

The American Philosophy of

Government

Back during my college days, I majored in both history and political science. When you think about it, most history is political in nature, so these were essentially two peas in the same academic pod. As young scholars in these two disciplines, we frequently were required to memorize the defining characteristics of the various forms of government; for example, Democracy, Republic, Theocracy, Monarchy, Oligarchy, Aristocracy, Dictatorship, Authoritarianism, etc. It was only after I escaped the oppression of the establishment educational system and continued my studies independently that I realized, for all practical purposes, there really have only been two types of government. By far, the most common —in fact the nearly universal—has been feudal kleptocracy.

"Feudal?!?" you may exclaim. "You're crazy. Feudalism ended centuries ago", you protest.

"What makes you think that?", I reply.

"Well, that's what they told me in school."

"I'm sure they did. They had reason to do so. In a feudal kleptocracy, the power elite uses the education system to keep you shrouded in the dark rather than basking in the light. Did you ever explore the topic of feudalism on your own, without the superintending guidance of the educational elite?"

If your answer is, "Uhhh, no", then you need to listen up.

Virtually every kleptocracy (I'll explain this term shortly) has worked to accomplish its goals by organizing itself along a feudal model. Under feudalism, a numerically small elite sits atop the power pyramid. Unfortunately for them, however, their numbers are insufficient to maintain control of the masses by themselves, and so they must enlist the aid of others. These "others" are the "vassals" whose loyalty is bought by the elite in various ways. In olden times the masters would secure the fidelity of the vassals by granting land holdings, titles of nobility, military rank, police powers, the ability to tax, etc. In more recent times the masters secure the fidelity of the vassals by granting preferential economic benefits, or other forms of enhanced influence, to the likes of big corporations, big unions, big media, big bankers — well, pretty much everything "big" because they didn't get and stay big without the blessings of those in power. Through these blessings, the vassals are given a vested interest in preserving the existing power structure and its elite leadership. Together, the elite and their vassals have enough power to coerce the masses into compliance. So, a feudal system is not some ancient model of government where the powerful are called kings and queens and lords and barons and dukes and duchesses and earls, etc. It is any form of government where a power elite buys the support of enough vassals to ensure their ability to control and steal from the masses. And this—the word "steal" in particular—brings me to explain what is a kleptocracy.

"Kleptocracy" comes from two Greek words: "klepto" which means "thief," and "crat" which means "rule." The English version of "crat" is "cracy." So, a "kleptocracy" is a ruling body, or government, that is organized to steal from others. When you look behind the flags and crests and pomp and circumstance of ruling bodies around the world and across the ages, you invariably find a den of thieves.

Throughout history, Kleptocrats have employed many of the same tactics in order to augment and preserve their power so they can successfully steal from the masses. Here are some of the most common.

    (1) They all seek to centralize and concentrate power in as few places as possible—preferably one. The people are much easier to manage that way.

    (2) They all seek to confiscate wealth, transferring it to themselves from the workers who created it. Wealth is the most versatile form of power, so the rulers want to appropriate it for themselves and deny it to others.

    (3) They all seek to minimize the liberties of the masses. Freedom makes people harder to control and more likely to rebel against the kleptocrats.

(4) They all seek to keep the masses disarmed or minimally armed. This denies the people the ability to fight back effectively.

(5) They all seek to keep the masses poorly educated. Knowledge is power which might be used against the governing elite.

(6) They often seek to encourage intoxication through alcohol or drugs. This is a good way to keep the people weak, disoriented, distracted, and unable to muster a successful revolt.

(7) They generally seek to undermine conventional ideas of morality and to redefine virtue so it works for their purposes. This enables the elite to sidestep accusations of immorality while claiming the moral high ground and smearing its opposition as depraved and disreputable.

Whenever you see politicians and bureaucrats working to accomplish these objectives, you know they are wittingly or unwittingly working for the power elite and against you. This is the litmus test for tyranny. Anything on this list sound familiar? Everything on this list sound familiar?

The one great exception to this nearly universal history of feudal kleptocracies has been the Constitutional Republic established along the eastern shore of North America in the late Eighteenth Century. This government deliberately sought to set the old model of governance on its head and bind the forces of feudal kleptocracy. Instead of concentrating and centralizing power, it deliberately dispersed it. Instead of confiscating wealth, it encouraged the people to create it and to keep it. Instead of crushing individual liberties, it guaranteed them. Instead of disarming the people, it promised the uninfringeable right to keep and bear arms. Instead of limiting and propagandizing the education of the people, it sought to universalize and broaden it. Instead of encouraging intoxication, it sought to limit the consumption of alcohol and forbid the use of dangerous drugs. Instead of crushing or perverting morality, it embraced it. Lo and behold, look what happened. History's strongest, wealthiest, noblest, and greatest nation was birthed. The phenomenon quickly caught the attention and the imagination of people around the world. Throngs flocked here to study the Great American Experiment and to join it.

However, as we might expect, the wealth and power created by the American juggernaut attracted the attention and avarice of others as well, both within and without her borders. Given the selfish nature of humankind, we should expect that so much power and wealth would come to be coveted by the power elite, and that they would conspire to subvert our system so they could control it. This is not some paranoid delusion of an unhinged conspiratorial theorist. This is Human Nature 101.

The United States presented the grandest brass ring in history. How could the unprincipled power elite resist such a prize? They couldn't. And so gradually, patiently, stealthily, they began their work to convert our grand Constitutional Republic into just another feudal kleptocracy—one which they controlled.

It has worked. The current structure of the American government, forged by both Democrats and Republicans, is not in the least what the Founders and Framers fought to create. They would be ashamed. So should we.

Some of you, no doubt, bristle at this analysis. You'd like to preserve that warm, fuzzy feeling you nurture about your rulers and their intentions. There is no space here to comprehensively rebut your faith, but think about this. Those rulers of yours tax everything from your income, to your property, purchases, utilities, gasoline, phones, motel visits, death, etc., etc., etc., and even rain water in some places. This all works to transfer the wealth that you create to the rulers' control, and virtually none of those taxes existed a little over a century ago. Those rulers impose regulations and attendant fees which transfer the wealth that you create to the rulers' control and which limit, shape, and steer our various activities to suit their purposes and reward their vassals who help secure their power and wealth. Virtually none of these regulations existed a little over a century ago. Those rulers shape fiscal and monetary policies and practices in ways that empower themselves and their allies and impoverish you. Virtually none of these fiscal and monetary policies and practices existed a little over a century ago. Those rulers have chiseled away at your fundamental rights and liberties. Those rulers have eroded your right to keep and bear arms which enables you to protect yourselves from them. More restrictions are planned for the near future. Those rulers have degraded the quality or our education and turned many schools into indoctrination centers which promote their agenda. Those rulers have promoted intoxication by lowering drinking ages, legalizing certain previously illegal drugs, turning a blind eye toward the misuse of other, dangerous legal drugs, and lessening the consequences for violating the laws we still do have in this area. Virtually none of these policies and practices existed a little over a century ago. Those rulers have eroded the influence and sources of traditional morality while substituting their own standards thereby allowing them to do as they please while calling their opponents reprobates. This is completely opposed to the way things were a little over a century ago.

Remember that litmus test for tyranny? It's turning bright red and blue. And for decades now it hasn't really mattered much whether the Republicans or the Democrats were sitting on the throne. Things keep getting better for them. Things keep getting worse for us, unless you are one of their vassals. They have changed the rules of the game so they cannot lose, and we cannot win.

So, what do we do now? Our options are clear. Resign yourself to defeat—or play a different game. But what game could that possibly be? Actually, we don't have to imagine it. We don't have to invent it. We merely have to remember it. We got it right before. So, let's do it again. But where do we start? At the beginning. The unique American miracle began with a unique American philosophy of government. Let's start there.

I suspect most Americans have no idea what is the American philosophy of government nor where it is defined. Let's test my theory. Can you state this philosophy and where it originated? I didn't mean to embarrass you, but this is something we really need to know, and the fact we don't is another article in the indictment of our educational system. It is time to correct that deficiency. Prepare to be wowed—not by me, but by the genius of our Founders and Framers and the source of American exceptionalism.

On July 2, 1776, the Second Continental Congress voted "That these United Colonies are, and of right ought to be, free and independent States, that they are absolved from all allegiance to the British Crown, and that all political connection between them and the State of Great Britain is, and ought to be, totally dissolved." On July 4, 1776, that same Congress voted to approve the legal document which justified that dissolution: the Declaration of Independence. (In fact, July 2 should probably be our real birthday. July 4 was just the day the birth certificate was stamped.)

The authors and authorizers of the Declaration wanted to do more than merely inform the British and the world that we would no longer be a part of their empire. We needed to justify our action—to enunciate why our relationship "ought to be, totally dissolved." In the course of doing that, we laid out our case. That case argued that the British Crown and Parliament had violated the most fundamental of laws; namely, the laws of nature and of nature's God. They broke the contract, so we were no longer obligated to honor it. In the course of this argument, the members of the Second Continental Congress had to define the purpose and function of government—the philosophy of government—which the British had violated. They did it in the second paragraph of the Declaration, and, oddly enough, the bulk of this brief and brilliant philosophy is recorded in the most-memorized portion of the Declaration: "We hold these truths to be self-evident, that all men are created equal, that they are endowed by their Creator with certain unalienable Rights, that among these are Life, Liberty and the pursuit of Happiness." Unfortunately, most people end their memory work there. Had they gone just ten words further, it might have dawned on them that this is a philosophy of government and not merely a collection of political platitudes. Those next ten words say, "That to secure these rights, Governments are instituted among Men...." Notice, the Declaration proclaims why governments are instituted, or created. That's a philosophy of government, and it becomes crystal clear if you read the key phrases in this package backwards. Here's what you get: "Governments are instituted among men to secure these rights that are endowed by their Creator." In other words, the rightful role of government is to do the work of God. The political work of God is "to secure these rights", the holy trinity of which are life, liberty, and property. Yes, I know the Declaration says "Life, Liberty and the pursuit of Happiness." That's quite strange. Most everywhere else the Founders—including Thomas Jefferson, the principle author of the Declaration—enumerate life, liberty, and property as the principle rights—and so have I.

This profound and simple philosophy—a mere fifteen words long —ignited a global phenomenon unlike anything ever seen in history. In order to understand why this concept is so unique and powerful, compare it with the philosophy that underlies all the feudal kleptocracies, which is "Governments are instituted among men to secure the power and privilege of the elite." Notice, in the ideology of the kleptocrats, there is no mention of God, no nod to morality, no protection of rights, no guarantees to the people—just a license to steal. Wow! No wonder the United States of America turned out so differently from the other nations of history. The goal of those nations was to serve the power elite. The goal of the United States was to serve God. The Founders did not stumble upon this idea. It was the spiritual and philosophical milk that had nourished them for generations. Consider these remarks from Gouverneur Morris, one of the men who signed the Declaration. "I believe that religion is the only solid basis of morals, and that morals are the only possible support of free governments." "The most important of all lessons from the Scriptures is the denunciation of the rulers of every state that rejects the precepts of religion. Those nations are doomed to death...." Doomed to death.

This philosophy of government was the guiding light which illuminated the path of those who crafted the Constitution eleven years later. Constitutions are similar to an architect's blueprint in that they not only describe how to construct a building but also how to maintain it. But an architect must begin with a concept. What is the purpose of the building and what is it suppose to accomplish? The design for a warehouse will be very different from the design for an outhouse. The guiding concept for the Framers of the Constitution was the philosophy of government specified in the Declaration. The Constitution was written in order to implement and institutionalize the philosophy of government presented in the Declaration. They built a government designed "to secure these rights that are endowed by their Creator." This means that there is a link between the Declaration and the Constitution that is strong and must remain indestructible. In another book of mine, *AR2; Handbook for the Second American Revolution*, I describe this concept as "Linkage."

There is a very important practical application for Linkage. Whenever the intent of the Constitution is unclear, go back to the Declaration. The Declaration provides the lens through which the Constitution must be read. The Declaration is the telescope through which we can clearly observe the overall purpose of the Constitution. It is the microscope through which we can accurately perceive the wisdom and direction of its finest details. Had we faithfully used that telescope, we never would have allowed the errant concept of "separation of church and state" to remove from government the very God it was supposed to be serving. We never would have allowed a warped understanding of "promote the general welfare" to be twisted so as to allow the violation of fundamental property rights and individual liberties. Had we consistently used that microscope, we never would have given a second thought to some perverse claim regarding a "right" to abortion--which violates the first and foremost right to life. Furthermore, the contention that there is a "right" to same-sex marriage would never have made it even to the county courthouse much less the Supreme Courthouse.

Let's take a closer look at the last two items—abortion and same-sex "marriage"—to see how Linkage could have prevented two very erroneous Supreme Court rulings and the horrific consequences that have resulted from them. In 1973 the U.S. Supreme Court case, Roe v. Wade, legalized abortion in the United States. The Court used a very twisted concept of privacy rights to come up with an opinion that even some liberal justices have called seriously flawed. Had the justices used Linkage, they would have started at the beginning and arrived at a very different conclusion. "We hold these truths to be self-evident, that all men are created equal…." We can stop right there. We already have the answer to whether abortion is a protected right. All people are created equal. This does not mean that they all are physically and intellectually equal, but that they are equal before the law. Everybody is entitled to the same enjoyment of rights and legal protections. But when does this equality begin? Does one have to be a certain age? Is it necessary to have completed a course, passed a test, and received a certificate of completion? Do you have to be so tall to ride this ride? The answer is in the Declaration. All people are "**created** equal." This means that from the moment of your creation you are entitled to the same equal protection of the law as everyone else, and your physical creation began at conception. Accordingly, the just conceived baby ("zygote" for those who seek to demean the value of the life in the womb) has the same rights as a one-year-old, a twenty-one year old, or a hundred-and-one year old. The most solemn and sacred responsibility of government is to "secure these rights", the preeminent of which is life. The Court got it wrong, and as of this writing, over sixty million innocent, helpless babies have been gruesomely slaughtered mostly for the sake of convenience. To my knowledge, not one had his or her legal rights observed as commanded by the Fourteenth Amendment.

And now on to same-sex "marriage." In 2015 the United States Supreme Court ruled in Obergefell v. Hodges that the fundamental right of marriage is guaranteed to same-sex couples based on the Due Process Clause and Equal Protection Claus of the Fourteenth Amendment of the Constitution. The argument was basically that if heterosexuals are allowed to do something, then homosexuals should also be allowed to do the same thing. That argument sounds conclusive until we use Linkage. Let's do that.

We return to that key passage defining our philosophy of government: "We hold these truths to be self-evident, that all men are created equal, that they are endowed by their Creator with certain unalienable Rights...." So, let's repeat and emphasize that rights come from God. Essentially, rights are something which God gives us permission to do. Do you really think God will give us permission to do something which He declares to be detestable, abhorrent, and an abomination? Not likely. This means that, accordingly to the American philosophy of government, no one has the right to do something that is contrary to the will and desires of God. The verdict, therefore, is clear. It doesn't matter whether one is talking about Jehovah or Allah (which the Founders wouldn't)-- it doesn't matter whether you turn to the Old Testament, the New Testament, or the Koran (which the Founders wouldn't)-- homosexual conduct is an "abomination" in the eyes of God. Accordingly, there is no right to homosexual marriage. Any court that rules otherwise is clearly wrong.

The Founders and Framers understood that their republic could not stand except upon the foundation of the Bible. They made this point over and over. We must remember and embrace it. We already quoted the remarks of Gouverneur Morris. Many others echoed this sentiment. Let's look at the thoughts of just one—the one who is primarily responsible for writing the Declaration, Thomas Jefferson. "Can the liberties of a nation be thought secure, when we have removed their only firm basis, a conviction in the minds of the people that these liberties are the gifts of God?—that they are not to be violated except with his wrath?"

Governments are instituted among men to secure these rights that are endowed by their Creator. There is a game called Jenga where wooden blocks are stacked and then deconstructed. Players try to remove a block at a time until the stack collapses. The winning contestant is the last player to remove a block without causing the stack to crash. God is the critical block in the structure of American government and society. Remove Him and the whole thing collapses. God was at the center of pretty much everything the Founders and Framers did. He was the foundation of pretty much everything they built. God is in our national DNA. He is our greatest strength. Should anyone ultimately succeed in removing Him from America, America will stop being America, and all will be lost.

Discussion

The author writes, *"a "kleptocracy" is a ruling body, or government, that is organized to steal from others. When you look behind the flags and crests and pomp and circumstance of ruling bodies around the world and across the ages, you invariably find a den of thieves."* When you stop and think about it, does this claim ring true, or sound far-fetched?

Review the seven tactics used by the kleptocrats to control the masses. Now, look at our own nation. Do you see these tactics being used today?

The author claims that *"one great exception to this nearly universal history of feudal kleptocracies has been"* the United States of America; and that this led to the founding of history's *"strongest, wealthiest, noblest, and greatest nation."* Can you see the connection between rejecting the tactics of the power elite and the rise of American greatness? Why do you think it worked out that way?

The Second Amendment, which established the right to keep and bear arms, was not included in the Bill of Rights in order to guarantee the people's ability to hunt or protect themselves from local criminals. It was included in the Bill of Rights to give the people the ability to protect themselves from national criminals, that is, the power elite. Have you noticed that many of the biggest opponents of the Second Amendment are also advocates of big government? Do you think that they are witting or unwitting agents of the power elite?

The author claims that *"we should expect that so much power and wealth would come to be coveted by the power elite, and that they would conspire to subvert our system so they could control it. This is not some paranoid delusion of an unhinged conspiratorial theorist. This is Human Nature 101."* Do you agree that humans, by nature, covet power and are often willing to resort to immoral means to gain great power? Name some examples. If this is true, do you believe a society must take measures to protect itself from a power elite amassing great power? How can they do that?

"The current structure of the American government, forged by both Democrats and Republicans, is not in the least what the Founders

and Framers fought to create. They would be ashamed. So should we." Do you agree that modern politicians have warped and even betrayed the ideals of our Founders and Framers? What do you think the consequences of this will be?

After detailing many ways in which the power elite has secured its power and wealth by denying yours, the author claims that *"for decades now it hasn't really mattered much whether the Republicans or the Democrats were sitting on the throne. Things keep getting better for them. Things keep getting worse for us, unless you are one of their vassals. They have changed the rules of the game so they cannot lose, and we cannot win."* Would you agree that even the members of your own party are complicit in this? Give some examples.

"I suspect most Americans have no idea what is the American philosophy of government nor where it is defined. Let's test my theory. Can you state this philosophy and where it originated?" What is the American philosophy of government? Where is it defined?

The author distinguishes the American philosophy of government (Governments are instituted among men to secure these rights that are endowed by their Creator) from the philosophy of the feudal kleptocracies which have dominated history (Governments are instituted among men to secure the power and privilege of the elite.) Who is the inspiration for the American philosophy? Who is the inspiration for the Kleptocrats' philosophy? Who benefits under the American philosophy? Who benefits under the Kleptocrats' philosophy? Under which form of government are the people more likely to be happy? Why? Under which form of government is revolt more likely to appear? Why? Where would you rather live: the American republic or a Kleptocracy? Why?

Describe the concept of "Linkage" as described by the author. Do you agree that the Constitution *"was written in order to implement and institutionalize the philosophy of government presented in the Declaration"*?

The author claims that both abortion and same-sex marriages are unconstitutional. Review his arguments for supporting these claims. Do you agree?

Thomas Jefferson asked, *"Can the liberties of a nation be thought secure, when we have removed their only firm basis, a conviction in the minds of the people that these liberties are the gifts of God?*

—that they are not to be violated except with his wrath?" Where are your liberties more secure; in a society where these liberties are believed to be "the gifts of God", or in a society where they are considered to be the gifts of the government? Why?

"God is the critical block in the structure of American government and society. Remove Him and the whole thing collapses." Removing God from "the structure of American government" may not end in the collapse of the United States; but, at a minimum, it would result in a very different kind of life for the citizens. Name some of the ways things would be different. Would you prefer to live in a Godless society or a Godly one? Why? Would that still be true if you were an atheist?

CHAPTER SEVEN:

Greatness Without Goodness?

John Adams, whose impressive historical resumé includes serving as the first vice-president and second president of the United States, once wrote that, "Our Constitution was made only for a moral and religious people. It is wholly inadequate to the government of any other." It's a great line, sure to get applause in a patriotic speech, but is it true, and if so, why?

I have often used a two-legged stool as a prop in presentations to conservative organizations to demonstrate a shortcoming of their political pronouncements and actions. I would start by pointing out that they tend to emphasize the need to protect personal liberties and shrink the size of government. These, I said, were the two main legs of their platform, but like a two-legged stool, it couldn't stand. I then tried to balance my stool on its two legs, which invariably failed. I went on to argue that the goals of preserving individual liberties and shrinking the size of government could only stand if they added a third leg: morality.

As much as we Americans—especially us traditional, conservative ones—like to talk about protecting and expanding liberties, this is NOT a good idea in every case. In fact, it can be spectacularly destructive. It cannot work without a moral society. Think about it. What do you suspect will happen if you grant a great deal of individual liberties to an immoral society? They will do immoral stuff, of course. And when you think about it, "immoral" invariably refers to selfish acts that hurt others without justification. So, granting a great deal of liberty to an immoral people will result in a lot of victims. It creates a society where only the bullies win. And if you add a weak government to administer such a society, then the bullies are unrestrained. Such a society cannot last long. The people—the victims—will become profoundly discontent and eventually will seek out the first strongman who promises safety. And so, the free but immoral society with a weak government will quickly devolve into tyranny.

Robert Charles Winthrop, a former Speaker of the House of Representatives, once observed that, "Men, in a word, must necessarily be controlled, either by a power within them, or by a power without them; either by the word of God, or by the strong arm of man; either by the Bible, or by the bayonet." The implications of this remark should be obvious. If you grant a great deal of personal liberty to a people who do not have a strong moral code which guides and constrains their behavior, they will use that liberty to pursue selfish objectives which victimize others. Under these circumstances, order and safety can only be established by the "strong arm" of government. So, if you want personal freedom and a limited government, you must first achieve morality, and morality is a creation of God. "But", you may protest, "great philosophers have also given us moral codes." No. They have given us opinions about how to construct a civil society which, at best, are transient and incomplete. God gives us eternal truths which stand the test of time and circumstances. Philosophers generally begin with man. Great moralists, including our Founders and Framers, began with God. Good beginnings lead to good endings—something we would be wise to remember.

John Jay, first Chief Justice of the United States Supreme Court, believed it is "the duty of all wise, free, and virtuous governments to countenance and encourage virtue and religion." Why? Because countenancing and encouraging virtue and religion are the only ways to achieve wise, free, and virtuous governments and societies. William Paterson, a signer of the Constitution and a Supreme Court Justice, backed up this idea when he wrote, "Religion and morality...[are] necessary to good government, good order, and good laws."

All this brings us back to Adams' remark that "Our Constitution was made only for a moral and religious people. It is wholly inadequate to the government of any other." The philosophy of government that is the foundation of our Constitution says that governments are instituted among men to secure these rights that are endowed by their Creator. Our government exists to "secure these rights" that protect individual liberty. But, as we have seen, a society which grants a great deal of individual liberty to an immoral people is destined to fail. And so we see the correctness of Adam's conclusion that our Constitution is wholly inadequate for a people who are not moral and religious.

Alexis Charles Henri Clérel, Comte de Tocqueville was born in 1805 into an aristocratic French family that had suffered during the upheavals of the French Revolution and Reign of Terror. He was a sociologist, political scientist, political philosopher, diplomat, and historian. In 1831 he and an associate traveled to the United States to study American prisons. He learned a great deal more, and after returning to France the next year, he began to write his observations about American politics and culture in a two-volume study entitled *Democracy in America,* the first volume of which was initially published in 1835. Among other things, de Tocqueville marveled at the important role our churches played in American society. He also fully appreciated the connection between the morality of a society and its stability and success. He wrote in *Democracy in America,* "Society is endangered not by the great profligacy of a few, but by the laxity of morals amongst all."

There is another famous remark attributed to de Tocqueville which may not be his. Regardless of its true origin, it is something de Tocqueville easily could have said, and is profound for its simplicity and its veracity. "America is great because she is good. If America ceases to be good, America will cease to be great." Commentators of all types have theorized about the strength of America. Some have noted our rich natural resources. Others have pointed to our economic wealth or military prowess. Actually, these are consequences of our greatness, not the causes of them. I would argue that the true fount of our greatness has been our devotion to God. As Washington said in his first inaugural address, "the propitious smiles of Heaven, can never be expected on a nation that disregards the eternal rules of order and right, which Heaven itself has ordained…." For most of our history, we did not disregard "the eternal rules of order and right, which Heaven itself has ordained" and so we were blessed to receive "the propitious smiles of Heaven." To put it another way, America was great because she was good. But things have changed in our relationship with God. Things have gotten much worse, and, not surprisingly, things also have changed in terms of our greatness. Everyone is worried, and with good reason. What happened and what can be done about it?

Discussion

John Adams wrote, "Our Constitution was made only for a moral and religious people. It is wholly inadequate to the government of any other." Do you believe that? Why or why not? If Adams is correct, what happens if we stop being "a moral and religious people"?

The author argues that *"the free but immoral society with a weak government will quickly devolve into tyranny."* Review his reasons for making that claim. Do you agree? If not, why not?

The author writes that *"if you want personal freedom and a limited government, you must first achieve morality, and morality is a creation of God."* What is the difference between God-based morality and man-based ethics? What is the objective of God's morality? What is the objective of man's ethics? Which is more likely to be eternal and which is more likely to be ephemeral? Where would you rather live?

PART TWO:

The Fall

"Woe to those who call evil good and good evil, who put darkness for light and light for darkness, who put bitter for sweet and sweet for bitter."

Isaiah 5:20

And the United States fell away from following the God

who had established them.

They rejected His teachings, turned from His pathways,

and committed a great sin.

CHAPTER EIGHT:

Stranger Things

In July, 2016, a horror mini-series was released called *Stranger Things*. A fictional small town in Indiana became the site of a portal which reached deep into a demonic underworld known as the Upside Down. "Upside down" is an apt description of what happens when demonic forces begin to infiltrate and overtake the Kingdom of God. The prophet Isaiah, described a salient aspect of such an infiltration more than seven centuries before the birth of Christ. He referred "to those who call evil good and good evil, who put darkness for light and light for darkness, who put bitter for sweet and sweet for bitter." [Isaiah 5:20] Many of us in America today can relate. "Things just seem crazy" is a common retort among rational and moral people. Think how quickly things have changed. Lifestyles we used to condemn or joke about are now celebrated and recognized with a month to honor them. Criminals are quickly returned to the streets, if they are arrested at all, leaving the law-abiding citizens vulnerable and endangered. And if that weren't bad enough, others talk about defunding the police, which would effectively eliminate our last civil bulwark against villainy and villains. News reporters describe "mostly peaceful protests" while city blocks are immolated in the background behind them. It used to be illegal to provide pornography to children. Now we pay school librarians to search it out, purchase it with our tax dollars, put it on the shelves of our public school libraries, and defend their actions when responsible parents complain. Politicians impose restrictions on the citizenry which they, themselves, violate whenever those restraints are inconvenient to them, or they think no one is watching. Values, opinions, and policies that have been respected and conventional throughout the vast majority of our history are now condemned as extremist. And while our value system has been turned upside-down, life in America is becoming unbearable. Crime is up. Homelessness is up. Sexual abuse is up. Human trafficking is up. Consumption of harmful drugs is up. Divorce and family disintegration are up. Uncertainty about the future is up. The only thing going down is America. God has been exiled from government. He has been expelled from our schools. Christianity, church attendance, and virtue in general are all declining. America has become a moral toxic waste dump.

Evil is always at work, so we should expect that America is in an on-going struggle against it. Until recently, however, we seemed to be winning, more or less. But in recent decades, it definitely has been less. The tide has shifted, and the forces of righteousness are definitely falling back. It would be useful to our understanding of this trend—and the methods of the enemy—if we could point to some event and some time when the retreat began. My vote for the time is 1947. The event: the United States Supreme Court case Everson v. Board of Education of the Township of Ewing.

Discussion

The author gave a list of areas where things have been getting worse in America. Can you add to that list?

The author believes that *"It would be useful to our understanding of this trend—and the methods of the enemy—if we could point to some event and some time when the retreat began."* What do you think precipitated this decline, and when did it start?

CHAPTER NINE:

Separation of God from

Government

April 8, 1966. For the first time in its history, *Time Magazine* featured a cover without a photograph. It had text only, and the blood-red letters read simply, "Is God Dead?" It was a question that had been unthinkable throughout the course of American history. Who could have imagined such a thing—and yet, there it was, in your face, as you passed the newsstand or gathered your mail. In fact, though, it probably spoke the unspeakable question on the minds of many Americans during that troubled decade. Drugs, hippies, counter-culture, the war in Vietnam, the sexual revolution, the prospect of nuclear Armageddon, riots, along with groups questioning, challenging, and revolting against the basic values of our country. This was a far cry from the calm of the Eisenhower's Fifties. We were the world's first superpower. Wasn't that suppose to guarantee us a healthy measure of calm and prosperity? What was happening? Who would save us? Where was God? A mere two decades earlier we basked in the glory of our victory against unadulterated evil. We had buried the Fascists, crushed the Nazis, and obliterated the Imperial Japanese war machine. We also had curbed the expansionist ambitions of our old ally, the Soviet Union. But now the stench of spiritual decomposition had begun to waft across the sweet land of liberty from sea to shining sea. What was happening? Who would save us? Where was God?

It seems as though America had pivoted, changing course fundamentally and quickly and with devastating consequences. If we could identify that fork in the road where we went so badly astray, it might help answer our previous questions: what was happening; who would save us; where was God. It also might help reveal what course correction we needed to make in order to fix things.

A New Jersey law had authorized local school boards to reimburse parents for the costs of transporting their children to and from schools, including private schools. About 96% of the private schools which benefitted from this law were Catholic. Arch R. Everson, a taxpayer in Ewing Township, filed a lawsuit alleging that this amounted to indirect aid to religion which violated both the New Jersey state constitution and the First Amendment of the federal Constitution. After losing in state courts, Everson appealed to the U.S. Supreme Court. The year was 1947. In a 5-4 decision, the Court held that the law did not violate the Constitution. Justice Hugo Black, who wrote the majority opinion, reasoned that the law did not pay money to parochial schools, nor did it support them directly in anyway. It was rather enacted to assist parents of all religions with getting their children to school.

So, it sounds like the good guys won. Unfortunately, Justice Black couldn't resist the temptation to pontificate and added the following comment: "The First Amendment has erected a wall between church and state. That wall must be kept high and impregnable. We could not approve the slightest breach." And thus was born the concept of "Separation of Church and State." But, Supreme Court justices don't get to just make up stuff and present it as a Constitutional principle. Surely Justice Black took this remark from the body of the Constitution or the Bill of Rights or a really reputable fortune cookie company, right? Nope. So, where did he get it?

After his election as President of the United States in 1800, Thomas Jefferson received a letter from a group of Baptists in Danbury, Connecticut. They congratulated him on his victory, and also expressed their hope that he would continue to be faithful to his reputation for protecting religious liberties. You see, the Baptists were not the large, dominant denomination back then that they are now. In fact, they were considered to be a little "fringy" by the other large congregations, and they feared persecution. Jefferson responded in January, 1802. He thanked the Danbury Baptists and sought to reassure them that he had their back. He wrote, "I contemplate with sovereign reverence that act of the whole American people which declared that their legislature should 'make no law respecting an establishment of religion, or prohibiting the free exercise thereof,' thus building a wall of separation between Church & State."

Justice Black was familiar with Jefferson's letter and incorporated it into his opinion. So, a brief remark in a private letter written by someone who was not involved in drafting the Constitution—who was not even in the country at the time it was written—has been elevated to the status of being the defining principle for rulings dealing with government and religion. Once Justice Black cracked open the door, the minions of evil stormed the gates with devastating consequences. It began an avalanche of other rulings that created an America that the Founders and Framers would not have recognized and would be ashamed of.

Here is a short list of the complaints that were lodged based on the erroneous notion of separation of church and state. Not all of these prevailed, but the list shows the depth of the devotion of evil to remove God from everything American.

Voluntary prayer in school—even by students praying over their own lunches—was challenged. Having a Bible in a school library or on a teacher's desk was questioned. The freedom of religious organizations to praise public school officials was disputed. Asking kindergartners whose birthday was celebrated at Christmas was allegedly objectionable. Having manger scenes in public parks was claimed to be unacceptable. Similarly, a cross-shaped planter at a public cemetery should not be tolerated. Images of the Ten Commandments in a courthouse or school were alleged to be forbidden. The words, "under God" in our Pledge of Allegiance and "In God we Trust" on our currency were claimed to be a violation of Constitutional law.

By the way, our national motto, "In God we Trust", is taken from the fourth verse of our national anthem, *The Star Spangled Banner*. Here it is.

> "O thus be it ever when freemen shall stand
>
> Between their lov'd home and the war's desolation!
>
> Blest with vict'ry and peace may the heav'n rescued land
>
> Praise the power that hath made and preserv'd us a nation!
>
> Then conquer we must, when our cause it is just,
>
> And this be our motto - "In God is our trust,"
>
> And the star-spangled banner in triumph shall wave

O'er the land of the free and the home of the brave."

Back to the complaints we considered above. Are any of these claims justified? The answer lies in the First Amendment, not an opinion of a Supreme Court justice. So, what does the First Amendment actually say regarding religion? "Congress shall make no law respecting an establishment of religion or prohibiting the free exercise thereof." There are two Constitutional principles expressed here. First, that Congress may not establish a formal, national religion, like the Church of England. Second, that Congress may not restrict the free exercise of religion. These prohibitions were later extended to the states as well.

Before going any further, let's note that no right is absolute. Generally speaking, a right may be limited or regulated when the exercise of that right begins to infringe upon another's freedom to exercise his rights, or when the exercise of a right grievously offends social norms. For example, I cannot kill someone and attempt to justify it by saying that my religion practices human sacrifice. The taking of innocent life definitely qualifies for infringing upon another's freedom to exercise his rights; namely, life. Regarding the egregious violation of accepted social norms, in 1879 the Supreme Court ruled unanimously in Reynolds v. United States that a federal law prohibiting polygamy—which was allowed by the Church of Latter Day Saints at the time—did not violate the free exercise clause. Polygamy was simply too objectionable to customary social mores and, so, could be regulated.

Now, back to the complaints lodged a few paragraphs back. Did any of those practices establish a state church? No. Did any of them prohibit the free exercise of a person's religion? No. Accordingly, they do not violate the Constitutional standards.

An argument has been made and often applied in these cases that some of these practices may influence others or make them feel uncomfortable about honoring their own religion. True, but the First Amendment does not say we are forbidden from doing anything that makes someone feel uncomfortable about practicing his or her religion. It says that we may not do anything that prohibits him or her from practicing his or her religion. A Supreme Court case in 1892, Church of the Holy Trinity v. United States, declared "this is a Christian nation." Well, if this is a Christian nation, you have to expect to see and hear Christian things; just like if you visit Germany, you have to expect to hear the German language.

I don't think that most of the Founders and Framers would have had a problem with separating the *institution* of the church from the *institution* of the state. They knew their history, and history had shown that the biggest abusers of personal liberties, the biggest organized criminals, and the biggest mass murderers were big government and big religion. Accordingly, they would have approved keeping these two institutions separated from one another in order to protect those precious liberties they had fought for during the eight-and-a-half years of the Revolution. However, we must make a distinction between the idea of separating the church and the state and the idea of removing God from government. The Founders and Framers never would have approved the latter idea, as we have already seen in earlier quotations from them. Let's refresh our memory with just one from John Adams. "Our Constitution was made only for a moral and religious people. It is wholly inadequate to the government of any other." Well, if our Constitution was made only for a moral and religious people, and we cease to be a moral and religious people, then our Constitutional government fails and falls. Obviously, the people who wrote the Constitution would not want that. Accordingly, they would want to affirm and support the survival of our Biblical society—and they said as much. Consider this remark from Oliver Ellsworth, the third Chief Justice of the United States Supreme Court, "The legislature, charged with the great interests of the community, may, and ought to countenance, aid, and protect religious institutions...the legislature may aid the maintenance of [Christianity], whose benign influence on morals is universally acknowledged. It may be added that this principle has been long recognized, and is too intimately connected with the peace, order, and happiness of the state to be abandoned."

To summarize, separating the institution of the church from the institution of the state is acceptable, indeed, required. Separating God from government is not acceptable, indeed, is suicidal. The God of the Bible is an integral part of the American story, the American culture, the American government, the American past, and the American future. Removing God from America is like removing wet from water or heat from fire. Those who have sought to remove God from government have perpetrated a perversion of the Constitution, not a preservation of it, and the consequences have been devastating.

Almost every personal and social problem we see in America has been caused or aggravated by "de-Godifying" our nation. Almost every personal and social problem we see in America would be solved or greatly improved by "re-Godifying" our nation. In a nutshell, that is what we need to do. What happens if we don't?

Discussion

The First Amendment's reference to religion states that "Congress shall make no law respecting an establishment of religion or prohibiting the free exercise thereof." The "Establishment Clause" is generally interpreted as forbidding the creation of a national church. The "Free Exercise Clause" states that the government is forbidden from denying people the freedom to worship as they choose, as long as their exercise of religion does not infringe upon the freedom of others nor is abhorrent to the social norms of the nation. Look again at the list of religious practices that have been challenged in court over the years. Do any of these activities violate either the Establishment Clause or the Free Exercise Clause?

Our national motto is "In God we Trust." Does this violate either the Establishment Clause or the Free Exercise Clause?

Some people have argued that having prayer in Congress, a Bible in a school library, and "In God we Trust" as our national motto constitute unconstitutional endorsements of religion. Do you agree? How would you argue your case based on the First Amendment?

The author claims that *"Almost every personal and social problem we see in America has been caused or aggravated by 'de-Godifying' our nation. Almost every personal and social problem we see in America would be solved or greatly improved by 're-Godifying' our nation."* Do you agree? Name a personal or social problem that did not result from removing God from our lives.

CHAPTER TEN:

Indictment

A loving God does what He wants. A righteous God does what He must.

Christians not only believe in Abba (papa or daddy), they also believe in Yahweh Tsidqenu (God of righteousness) and Adonai (Lord and Master). The loving Father longs to bless His children. The righteous Lord and Master has the duty to chastise and correct them when they go astray. A righteous God cannot ignore iniquity and sin. He simply cannot look the other way, or shrug His shoulders, or dismiss wickedness saying "Boys will be boys." If God ignores sin, He not only loses His claim to righteousness, He loses His righteousness, and God simply cannot do that. Even though the loving Abba might want to let bygones be bygones, the God of righteousness cannot. Accordingly, we must expect some form of correction when we sin. Granted, Jesus died to save us, but salvation and judgment are not the same things. There must be consequences for sin here on Earth whether God likes the idea or not. Imagine the coach who is disappointed in his team's lackluster performance. He might forgive them—and then tell them to run a lap.

There are consequences for our disobedience, and that applies to nations as well as individuals. The once-faithful United States has sinned—grievously. It calls "evil good and good evil"; it puts "darkness for light and light for darkness"; it puts "bitter for sweet and sweet for bitter." [Isaiah 5:20] What will likely be the consequences for us? We don't have to imagine. This story has been told before. Our future is revealed in the past.

Here is a timeline for a portion of the history of the nation of Israel. At or around 1451 B.C. Joshua led the nation in the occupation of the Promised Land. From about 1425 B.C—1095 B.C. we have the Age of Judges. This is followed by the first chapter of the Kingdom of Israel under the reigns of King Saul, King David, and King Solomon. In or about 931 B.C. King Solomon died, and the Kingdom is divided. In 722 B.C. the

Assyrians finish their conquest of the Northern Kingdom also known as Israel and Samaria. In 586 or 587 B.C. the Babylonians crush the Southern Kingdom of Judah. In 538 B.C. Cyrus (founder of the first Persian Empire) allows the Jews to return to Jerusalem. In particular we will examine the period of the Divided Kingdom from 931 B.C. to 586 B.C.

King Solomon was succeeded by his son, Rehoboam. Most of us who ever went to Sunday school know that Solomon was known for his great wisdom. He's the one who ordered the baby to be cut in half in order to figure out which of the two claimants was the real mother—remember? Well, things didn't go so well for Solomon later in life, as is explained in the eleventh chapter of 1 Kings.

> "King Solomon, however, loved many foreign women besides Pharaoh's daughter—Moabites, Ammonites, Edomites, Sidonians and Hittites. They were from nations about which the Lord had told the Israelites, 'You must not intermarry with them, because they will surely turn your hearts after their gods.' Nevertheless, Solomon held fast to them in love. He had seven hundred wives of royal birth and three hundred concubines, and his wives led him astray. As Solomon grew old, his wives turned his heart after other gods, and his heart was not fully devoted to the Lord his God, as the heart of David his father had been. He followed Ashtoreth the goddess of the Sidonians, and Molek the detestable god of the Ammonites. So Solomon did evil in the eyes of the Lord; he did not follow the Lord completely, as David his father had done. [1 Kings 11:1-6, NIV]

Well, as you might imagine, God was not too happy about this. In fact, you don't have to imagine. Let's continue the story, starting with verse 9.

> "The Lord became angry with Solomon because his heart had turned away from the Lord, the God of Israel, who had appeared to him twice. Although he had forbidden Solomon to follow other gods, Solomon did not keep the Lord's command. So the Lord said to Solomon, 'Since this is your attitude and you have not kept my covenant and my decrees, which I commanded you, I will most certainly tear the kingdom away from you and give it to one of your subordinates. Nevertheless, for the sake of David your father, I will not do it during your

lifetime. I will tear it out of the hand of your son. Yet I will not tear the whole kingdom from him, but will give him one tribe for the sake of David my servant and for the sake of Jerusalem, which I have chosen.'" [1 Kings 11:9—13]

Sure enough, upon Solomon's death, his son, Rehoboam, became king. Something like a tribal council followed where the new king was asked if he planned to continue his father's practice of abusive taxation. Rehoboam sought advice from a group of older counselors (who told him to take it easy on the people) and some young bucks (who advised Rehoboam to show the people who's boss and increase the levies.) Unfortunately, Rehoboam followed the advise of his youthful advisers, the people revolted, and most of the tribes of Israel abandoned him. Meanwhile, God had prepared for this divided kingdom by appointing and anointing a new king for the north. He sent a prophet, Ahijah, to inform one of Solomon's project managers, Jeroboam, about his good fortune.

"'See, I am going to tear the kingdom out of Solomon's hand and give you ten tribes. But for the sake of my servant David and the city of Jerusalem, which I have chosen out of all the tribes of Israel, he will have one tribe. I will do this because they have forsaken me and worshiped Ashtoreth the goddess of the Sidonians, Chemosh the god of the Moabites, and Molek the god of the Ammonites, and have not walked in obedience to me, nor done what is right in my eyes, nor kept my decrees and laws as David, Solomon's father, did." [1 Kings 11:31-33]

God then made a promise to Jeroboam. "If you do whatever I command you and walk in obedience to me and do what is right in my eyes by obeying my decrees and commands, as David my servant did, I will be with you. I will build you a dynasty as enduring as the one I built for David and will give Israel to you. I will humble David's descendants because of this, but not forever.'" [1 Kings 11:38—39] That sounds like a pretty good deal, but Jeroboam did not follow God's commands, and neither did any of his successors. Israel, also known as Samaria, had 19 kings, all of whom "did what was evil in the sight of the Lord." Despite repeated warnings, the people of the north continued their evil ways—and God noticed.

"Jeroboam enticed Israel away from following the Lord and caused them to commit a great sin. The Israelites persisted in all the sins of Jeroboam and did not turn away from them until the

> Lord removed them from his presence, as he had warned through all his servants the prophets. So the people of Israel were taken from their homeland into exile in Assyria...." [2 Kings 17:21—23]

The Assyrian kingdom was founded in northern Mesopotamia, located in modern-day Iraq and southeastern Turkey. It started as a city-state back in the twenty-first century B.C. Around the fourteenth century B.C. it became a nation and then an empire until the seventh century B.C. During its expansion to the south and west, around 740 B.C., Assyria confronted and conquered the Israelite tribes east of the Jordan River; namely, the Reubenites, the Gadites, and the half-tribe of Manasseh. The tribes west of the Jordan agreed to pay tribute to avoid a similar fate. Eventually, the western tribes refused to continue paying tribute, and after a three-year siege, the remaining tribes of Israel were conquered around 722 B.C. The area was looted and many people were carried off into exile.

Why would God allow such a thing to happen to His chosen people? Many of the verses in the seventeenth chapter of 2 Kings amount to God's indictment of the Israelites as well as an explanation for His actions.

> "They rejected his decrees and the covenant he had made with their ancestors and the statutes he had warned them to keep. They followed worthless idols and themselves became worthless. They imitated the nations around them although the Lord had ordered them, 'Do not do as they do.' They forsook all the commands of the Lord their God and made for themselves two idols cast in the shape of calves, and an Asherah pole. They bowed down to all the starry hosts, and they worshiped Baal. They sacrificed their sons and daughters in the fire. They practiced divination and sought omens and sold themselves to do evil in the eyes of the Lord, arousing his anger. So the Lord was very angry with Israel and removed them from his presence." [2 Kings 17:15—18]

These verses in 2 Kings 17 not only constitute an indictment, I fear it is safe to say that they also provide a template for righteous retribution. They point out exactly what can be expected from God among the peoples who abandon Him.

Allow me to repeat the verses from 2 Kings 17:21—23. "Jeroboam enticed Israel away from following the Lord and caused them to commit a great sin. The Israelites persisted in all the sins of Jeroboam and did not turn away from them until the Lord removed them from his presence, as he had warned through all his servants the prophets." Now allow me to alter the wording a bit to illustrate a point. "The leaders of the United States enticed America away from following the Lord and caused them to commit a great sin. The Americans persisted in all the sins of their leaders and did not turn away from them until the Lord removed them from his presence, as he had warned through all his servants the prophets."

Does that seem a bit dramatic? Well, what else can we expect? Do you think the righteous God will see what we have done and simply look the other way, or shrug His shoulders, or dismiss wickedness saying "Boys will be boys"? That's what the Southern Kingdom of Judah hoped. If you know the story, you know it didn't work out very well for them either. The account in 2 Kings 17 picks up where we left off with verse 18. "Only the tribe of Judah was left, and even Judah did not keep the commands of the Lord their God. They followed the practices Israel had introduced. " [2 Kings 17:18—19] God's indictment of the Southern Kingdom is recorded in Jeremiah.

> "the people aroused my anger by burning incense on the roofs to Baal and by pouring out drink offerings to other gods. The people of Israel and Judah have done nothing but evil in my sight from their youth; indeed, the people of Israel have done nothing but arouse my anger with what their hands have made, declares the Lord. From the day it was built until now, this city has so aroused my anger and wrath that I must remove it from my sight." [Jeremiah 32:29—31]

If you have been attending church services very long, you undoubtedly have heard a pastor tell you to pay particular attention whenever God says something twice. God used the word "anger" three times in the passage above. He is ticked. And the indictment continues.

> "The people of Israel and Judah have provoked me by all the evil they have done—they, their kings and officials, their priests and prophets, the people of Judah and those living in Jerusalem. They turned their backs to me and not their faces; though I taught them again and again, they would not listen or respond to discipline. They set up their vile images in the house that bears my Name and defiled it. They built high places for Baal

> in the Valley of Ben Hinnom to sacrifice their sons and daughters to Molek, though I never commanded—nor did it enter my mind—that they should do such a detestable thing and so make Judah sin." [Jeremiah 32:32—35]

What do you suppose God is going to do—look the other way, shrug His shoulders, dismiss it all by saying "Boys will be boys"? No. He did that which the Israelites considered unthinkable. God used His template of righteousness and even destroyed the Temple.

> "This is the word that came to Jeremiah from the Lord in the tenth year of Zedekiah king of Judah, which was the eighteenth year of Nebuchadnezzar...'This is what the Lord says: I am about to give this city into the hands of the king of Babylon, and he will capture it. Zedekiah king of Judah will not escape the Babylonians but will certainly be given into the hands of the king of Babylon, and will speak with him face to face and see him with his own eyes. He will take Zedekiah to Babylon, where he will remain until I deal with him, declares the Lord. If you fight against the Babylonians, you will not succeed.'" [Jeremiah 32:1,3—5]

Pause a moment to ponder the hopelessness of that last line. God, Himself, tells His people to just give up. They cannot win. We had a saying in the Marines that if you hurt the United States and we are sent to deal with you, you may as well just give up. If you run or fight, you'll just die tired. I think I know where we got that saying: Jeremiah 32:5.

The lessons taught by God, Himself, are powerful and brutal. Don't miss them. Among other things, God teaches that the consequences of sin are not just personal—they are national. God does not just hold individuals responsible for their behavior. He also holds whole nations responsible as well. He blesses and punishes them accordingly. Our Founders understood this. Remember the words of George Washington in his first Inaugural Address: "The propitious smiles of Heaven can never be expected on a nation that disregards the eternal rules of order and right, which Heaven itself has ordained." In other words, if you don't do it God's way, don't expect God to do it your way. Don't expect God to bless America if America refuses to bless God.

Nor will God just judge and punish the leaders. If the people follow evil leaders—if they even tolerate them—the people will share their fate.

"Jeroboam enticed Israel away from following the Lord and caused them to commit a great sin. **The Israelites** persisted in all the sins of Jeroboam and did not turn away from them until the Lord removed them from his presence...." [2 Kings 17:21—23 Emphasis added] "**They** rejected his decrees and the covenant he had made with their ancestors and the statutes he had warned them to keep. **They** followed worthless idols and themselves became worthless. **They** imitated the nations around them although the Lord had ordered them, 'Do not do as they do.' **They** forsook all the commands of the Lord their God and made for themselves two idols cast in the shape of calves, and an Asherah pole. **They** bowed down to all the starry hosts, and **they** worshiped Baal. **They** sacrificed their sons and daughters in the fire. **They** practiced divination and sought omens and sold themselves to do evil in the eyes of the Lord, arousing his anger." [2 Kings 17:15—17 Emphasis added]

And still another important lesson tucked away in 2 Kings 17:15: "They followed worthless idols and themselves became worthless." You are only as good as what you worship. So, pause a moment to consider who or what do you worship—wealth, fame, power, ease of living, self? Who or what do we worship as a nation? What are our idols? The donkey? The elephant? Who are our idols? Reagan, Clinton, Obama, Trump? Where is God and the Godly on these lists?

And what about our national policies and practices? Abortion, sexualization of children, taking pride in what God calls abomination, sexual immorality, crime and violence, softening position on drugs, official theft of wealth, sympathy for Islam, "separation of church and state", weakening of Christian values and practices, etc.

How do you think God feels about this? What can you expect Him to do? Don't guess. Remember. "Because the Lord was very angry with Israel, [America?] he swept them away from his presence."

It is precisely at times like these that we, the people, need strong, decisive, wise, and Godly leadership. It is precisely because we, the people, have not had this leadership that we are in the current mess. Who is responsible for our failure? Many answers may come to mind, but an observation by a nineteenth century pastor may be the most accurate, compelling, and damning.

Pastor Charles Finney (1792—1875) was a champion of the Second Great Spiritual Awakening in America. He laid responsibility for spiritual decay squarely upon the shoulders of our pastors, preachers, and priests.

He wrote, "If there is a decay of conscience, the pulpit is responsible for it. If the public press lacks moral discernment, the pulpit is responsible for it. If the church is degenerate and worldly, the pulpit is responsible for it. If the world loses its interest in Christianity, the pulpit is responsible for it. If Satan rules in our halls of legislation, the pulpit is responsible for it. If our politics become so corrupt that the very foundations of our government are ready to fall away, the pulpit is responsible for it."

How could a man who died a century-and-a-half ago describe the situation in America today so precisely? Because the objectives and tactics of evil do not change much from age to age, and evil is afoot in the land today. We have been conditioned to turn to the politicians for solutions to all our problems. That is a grave mistake and may prove to be a fatal one. Politicians are often the witting or unwitting agents of evil; which means that politics is often the field upon which the forces of evil unfold their plans. And yet, our spiritual "leaders" often tell us to surrender that field. In the next chapter, we will consider their reasons for doing this, and why they are so wrong.

Discussion

The author opens the chapter with *"A loving God does what He wants. A righteous God does what He must."* What does he mean by this?

"If God ignores sin, He not only loses His claim to righteousness, He loses His righteousness, and God simply cannot do that." Do you agree? Can God retain His righteousness if He allows sin to continue unabated and unpunished? Wouldn't that make Him a collaborator in sin?

"There are consequences for our disobedience, and that applies to nations as well as individuals." Have you ever thought about the fact that nations may suffer for the sins of its citizens? Do you think that is just? Why or why not?

The author paraphrased verses in 2 Kings 17:21—23 like this: *"The leaders of the United States enticed America away from following the Lord and caused them to commit a great sin. The Americans persisted in all the sins of their leaders and did not turn away from them until the Lord removed them from his presence, as he had warned through all his servants the prophets."* Do you think this is a possibility? What would it look like if "the Lord removed [us] from his presence"? Would you want to live in such a place?

The people of Judah in the south were aware of what happened in the Northern Kingdom of Israel, and yet they continued to ignore God. Why would someone do this?

Recall the author's opening remark that a righteous God does what He must. Is this confirmed in Jeremiah 32:31 where God says, *"From the day it was built until now, this city has so aroused my anger and wrath that I <u>must</u> remove it from my sight."*? [Emphasis added]

"Among other things, God teaches that the consequences of sin are not just personal—they are national. God does not just hold individuals responsible for their behavior. He also holds whole nations responsible as well. He blesses and punishes them accordingly." Does this make you more determined to rise against the evil being committed by our national leaders?

The author also writes, *"Nor will God just judge and punish the leaders. If the people follow evil leaders—if they even tolerate them—the people will share their fate."* If this is true, we can take no comfort in the knowledge that we, personally, did not commit a great sin. Maybe you never had an abortion. Maybe you never engaged in homosexual acts. But what have you done to fight back against these things which God detests?

"'They followed worthless idols and themselves became worthless.' You are only as good as what you worship. So, pause a moment to consider who or what do you worship…." Please do that. What do you worship? What do you put before God? Do you ever, in effect, say, "Not now, God. There's something else more important than your way that I want to pursue"? Do you think anything you can come up with for your life will be better than what God has come up with?

The author asks, "Who is responsible for our failure" and then quotes Pastor Charles Finney:

"If there is a decay of conscience, the pulpit is responsible for it. If the public press lacks moral discernment, the pulpit is responsible for it. If the church is degenerate and worldly, the pulpit is responsible for it. If the world loses its interest in Christianity, the pulpit is responsible for it. If Satan rules in our halls of legislation, the pulpit is responsible for it. If our politics become so corrupt that the very foundations of our government are ready to fall away, the pulpit is responsible for it."

Do you agree with Finney? Is it because of the failure of the church and its leaders that we find ourselves in a position of voting for the lesser evil instead of the greater righteousness?

In more recent times, James Garlow and David Barton write, "America is in deep trouble primarily because the Church in America today has become largely impotent and irrelevant—it no longer functions collectively as salt and light and is neither a preservative in the culture nor a guiding beacon for the nation to follow." [*This Precarious Moment*, Salem Books 2018, P. 216] If the church is no longer a preservative, then will the heritage of America be saved? If the church no longer provides a "guiding beacon for the nation to follow", who or what will; and where will that lead?

The author writes, *"We have been conditioned to turn to the politicians for solutions to all our problems. That is a grave mistake and may prove to be a fatal one."* Do you agree? Well, if we do not turn to the politicians to solve our problems, to whom should we turn?

CHAPTER ELEVEN:

Keep Out!

Martin Luther once wrote, "Even the Devil is God's Devil." Satan does not have free rein. He is constrained and restrained by God. God allows him some leeway, but, ultimately, has him on a leash. Satan doesn't get to dine at the banquet table. He has to make due with the scraps that fall on the floor.

Satan needs power to continue the ambitions of his rebellion, and God doesn't allow him all he wants or needs. He forever is seeking more, because power is the ability to achieve, and without it, you simply cannot achieve. So, where would Satan look to find more power? Well, where are the greatest concentrations of power on Earth? Capitals, where the politics of a people play out. Politics is primarily about power—how it is acquired, how it is distributed, and how it is exercised. And for this reason, you can always expect Satan to be involved in politics. So, what happens if the righteous stay out of politics? Satan wins. And this is precisely what the righteous are suppose to prevent. How do we do this by staying out of politics?

If you had to pick one verse from Scripture to describe Jesus' mission statement, which verse would that be? My vote goes to 1 John 3:8, "The reason the Son of God appeared was to destroy the devil's work." As followers of Christ, this must be our mission as well: to destroy the works of the Devil. But as any good—or even mediocre—general knows, you cannot engage an enemy unless you go where he is. If Satan is engaged heavily in the political arena, then that is where we must go. It seems pretty obvious, but why, then, do so many Christian misleaders refuse to talk about political matters? Why do they tell their flocks to stay out of politics? Can you think of a better formula for failure? Doesn't this allow Satan to control the field of battle uncontested—unmolested? We will spend the remainder of this chapter considering and debunking the main reasons our errant shepherds have used to stay out of politics.

Separation of church and state. Some of our Christian misleaders have bought into this noxious notion and use it as a reason to avoid political action. We already discussed this at some length in Chapter Nine. The concept of "separation of church and state" is poorly understood and wrongly applied. It is a perversion of Constitutional principles, not a preservation of them.

Loss of the church's tax-exempt status. Back in 1954 Lyndon Baines Johnson, then a United States Senator, supported a change in the federal tax code that would prohibit all 501(c)(3) non-profit organizations, like churches, from endorsing or opposing political candidates. It almost certainly is unconstitutional and has only been used once or twice. Despite this, it sent a debilitating shiver down the squishy spines of a huge number of pastors, and coerced them into silence. Any pastor who is more concerned about losing the freedom to rake in tax-free donations than with standing up to evil needs to resign. He or she is obviously unfit to do the job. We used to have courageous leaders who would rather die miserably to destroy the works of the devil than to let evil gain an inch of the Master's ground. Where are they now? Get in the fight. God can provide far more than your parishioners.

Politics is dirty. Yes, it often is, but is that grounds for staying away? I'm sure glad Jesus didn't think like that. If He had, we'd all be going to Hell. Jesus came here precisely because it was dirty. That's where the need was. That's where the job was. It still is. He marched boldly into the filth and muck, and if you aspire to be His follower, guess where that will lead you.

Jesus was not political. For those of you who receive Christmas cards, it is a pretty safe bet that you have received one or more with the verse from Isaiah 9:6: "For unto us a child is born, unto us a son is given…." Please notice the little dots after the word "given." There is more to the verse. It goes like this,

> "For unto us a child is born, unto us a son is given: and the government shall be upon his shoulder: and his name shall be called Wonderful, Counsellor, The mighty God, The everlasting Father, The Prince of Peace. Of the increase of his government and peace there shall be no end, upon the throne of David, and upon his kingdom, to order it, and to establish it with judgment and with justice from henceforth even for ever." [Isaiah 9:6—7 KJV]

Notice, "the government shall be on his shoulder...his government...his kingdom...." That sounds political. But it also sounds far into the future. What about during Jesus' time on Earth? Was He political then? Consider this.

For whom did Jesus reserve some of His harshest criticisms? The members of the Sanhedrin and their agents; and not only were they the religious leaders of Judea during the first century, they also constituted a political body.

The word "Sanhedrin" is a combination of two Greek words which mean, "seated together." They were a ruling assembly or council consisting of seventy-one members with the High Priest as the chief officer. The number of members is thought to have come from God's direction to Moses recorded in Numbers 11:16—17.

"The Lord said to Moses: 'Bring me seventy of Israel's elders who are known to you as leaders and officials among the people. Have them come to the tent of meeting, that they may stand there with you. I will come down and speak with you there, and I will take some of the power of the Spirit that is on you and put it on them. They will share the burden of the people with you so that you will not have to carry it alone.'"

Regarding the claim that the Sanhedrin was a political body as well as a religious one, remember that, once they conquered a region, the Romans often turned to local leaders to manage the territory thereafter. If you look at a map of the Roman Empire at this time, you cannot help but be amazed at how they managed such a large area without modern communications and administrative tools. The Romans had developed a very effective procedure for expanding and controlling their empire. First, they would overwhelm a territory with their legions. They then terrorized the local populace by crucifying huge numbers—sometimes thousands —of those who resisted the Roman conquest and leadership. They then offered a deal to the surviving elements of the old regime. Run things for us, and we'll let you keep your privileged positions and lifestyle—or, go to the cross. After finding enough compliant Quislings, they left a small detachment of legionaries to ensure the fidelity of the local leaders while the rest of the Romans went on to new conquests or a comfortable retirement on the loot they had pillaged. The compliant Quislings in Judea at the time of Jesus were the members of the Sanhedrin. Accordingly, the Sanhedrin was political, Jesus did contend with them, and they ultimately sent

Him to the cross—with the permission of the Roman governor. Conclusion: yes, Jesus was political.

Romans 13. "Let everyone be subject to the governing authorities, for there is no authority except that which God has established. The authorities that exist have been established by God. Consequently, whoever rebels against the authority is rebelling against what God has instituted, and those who do so will bring judgment on themselves." [Romans 13:1—2]

Many pastors have stumbled over this verse and caused countless others to fall face down along with them. Still, it's easy to see how it happened. The meaning of the verses seems clear, though baffling. There have been many, many evil leaders throughout history and in our own personal lives. Why would a righteous God want us to yield to evil leaders? He wouldn't. But it says…. I know what it says. Do you know what it means? Everything hinges—rises or falls—on the meaning of one word, and this is the word which trips up those stumbling pastors I mentioned above. Strangely, I received my illumination on this passage from a very secular source.

As I mentioned earlier, during my undergraduate days I majored in both political science and history. Power is the underlying theme of both history and political science. It should not be surprising, therefore, that we novice scholars would quickly be introduced to that topic.

I clearly remember the lecture of one of my professors on this subject. He explained that throughout history, most dominion has been based on brutality. Brute force is the thread that has woven the fabric of history. That should come as no surprise. Those of us who had older siblings learned that lesson while still in diapers. And if we had not learned this lesson by the time we went to school, it was quickly taught on the playground. Who determined what game everyone else played during recess? The one who was the biggest, strongest, and most aggressive. On the playground, the one with the biggest biceps wins. On the fields of history, the one with the strongest steel, the most tanks, and the biggest army wins.

Here's your history lesson for the day. The farmer with the most farmhands who are trained and equipped to fight becomes the local warlord. The local warlord who has the biggest militia that is trained and equipped to fight becomes the king. The king who has the biggest and best equipped army becomes the emperor. That is the history of nation-building. Everything else are mere details.

However, my professor explained, there is another type of dominion—or rule—that is not founded upon brutality. It is legitimate power and is called "authority." Although authority needs to have brute force available to it, or it likely won't last long in this world, it is not founded upon brute force. Authority has a higher calling. To understand the nature of authority and its distinction from brute force, it is helpful to notice the root word of authority, which is, "author." The legitimacy of an "authority" is not based upon brute force. It is based upon compliance with and obedience to the author. An authority reigns to serve and accomplish the objectives of the author.

Authors do not have to be human. In fact, throughout history, the authors of authority often are not human, but rather something greater. Probably the three most common authors down through the ages have been tradition (from which we get common law), acceptance of some nearly universally honored principles or document which expresses those principles (like the Magna Carta or the American Constitution), and the divine (God).

So, here's the critical distinction for our present discussion. Not all rulers, administrators, supervisors, officials, etc. are authorities. One is **only** an authority if one faithfully serves the author, and one is only an authority **while** one is serving the author. Just being the boss or the mayor or the governor or the president does not make one an authority. It doesn't matter if the boss has a brass nameplate on his desk, even if it is the Resolute Desk in the Oval Office of the White House. If the boss does not serve the author, he or she is not an authority. If a boss used to serve the author but then stops, he or she ceases to be an authority.

I think it is a pretty safe bet that of the three types of authors mentioned above, Paul was referring to God in his letter to the Romans. So, when he writes, "Let everyone be subject to the governing authorities", he is saying that we should only subject ourselves to the governing officials who are faithfully serving God. What about those who do not faithfully serve God—or another author, like the Constitution? Then we are not obligated to serve that official. In fact, we are obligated to resist that official and all who work for him. When government officials command what God forbids, or forbid what God commands, they are **not** authorities.

We are obligated to obey God—**always**. We are obligated to disobey the ungodly **always**—even violently if necessary.

If we were inclined to give our errant pastors a little grace, we might excuse their errancy on the fact that most of them probably do not have a degree in political science and, accordingly, would not understand the fine points about the meaning of the word "authority." However, I am afraid I cannot grant that grace. If you make your living with words—especially if you use those words to instruct and edify others for the glory of God—then you had better understand the meaning of the words you use. Our misinforming misleaders goofed, and untold thousands have been led astray. Of course guys like Hitler, Stalin, Mao, Castro, Amin, and many others (including some much closer to us in terms of time and space) would be grateful to these errant pastors for neutering the Christian populations in their nations. Nor can we excuse our pastors on the suspicion they may have used a version of the Bible that did not translate Paul's passage using the word "authority." Almost all modern translations use the word "authority" in these verses. NIV, NRSV, NKJV, NASB, NLT, NAB, HCSB, for example, all use the same word: "authority." Only the King James Version, among the other popular translations of today, departs from this practice, using the expression "higher powers." I know this version is passionately popular among many Christians, but it is not highly rated among many modern scholars. After all, it did add the doxology ("For thine is the kingdom, and the power, and the glory, for ever") to the Lord's Prayer—words that are not in the original text.

But even if we did give these misleading pastors a pass on misunderstanding the word "authority", how did they miss the obvious contradiction between their instruction—to just suck it up when we suffer under ungodly leaders—and the numerous examples in the Bible where God rewards rebellion against evil leaders? Here are a few examples. The Hebrew midwives who disobeyed Pharaoh's order to kill all the newborn Jewish baby boys. Moses thumbs his nose at Pharaoh and leads a rebellion to free the Israelites. Many of the judges who fought against foreign rulers as recorded in the book of *Judges*. Elijah's ongoing fight against Ahab and Jezebel. Shadrach, Mechack, and Abednego who refused to bow before the golden statue. Daniel who prayed despite Darius's order. The apostles of Jesus who continued to preach about their Master despite the Sanhedrin's order to desist. Paul's repeated defiance against governing officials. And the command in James 4:7 to "Resist the Devil" even though he is called "the ruler of this world" more than once.

To sum up, only those officials who faithfully obey the "author" are "authorities", and the ultimate author is God. When Paul writes "Let everyone be subject to the governing authorities" he is saying that we should only subject ourselves to those who faithfully follow God. As for all others, when government officials command what God forbids, or forbid what God commands, they are **not** authorities. Allow me to repeat something I wrote earlier: We are obligated to obey God—**always**. We are obligated to disobey the ungodly **always**—even violently if necessary.

Turn the other cheek. Politics is often contentious, and the Bible tells us to avoid contention, doesn't it? That's what a lot of Christian misleaders tell us, right? Well, for the moment, let's just forget about all those times God orders His people to contend with others—even to the point of killing every last one of them. Let's give the Christian misleaders their day—or, at least, a few moments—and consider a few verses they use to argue that we should avoid contention and, therefore, politics because politics is so contentious.

One of their favorite verses is Matthew 5:39, repeated in Luke 6:29, which admonishes us to turn the other cheek. In the same chapter which records Jesus' "Sermon on the Mount", we read this, "If anyone slaps you on the right cheek, turn to them the other cheek also." Some go so far as to interpret this to be a general prohibition against fighting altogether. Let's be as careful in interpreting the words of Jesus as, I'm sure, He was careful in selecting those words.

First of all, isn't it interesting that Jesus specifically designated the "right" cheek? Let's dig into this a bit. Most opportunities to slap another, or to be slapped by another, would be in a face-to-face confrontation. The vast majority of people are right handed, and so would probably use their right hands to slap another. But if you, a right-handed person, attempt to slap a person facing you, aren't you most likely to hit their left cheek? The only way to engage that person's right cheek—without walking behind him—would be with a backhand stroke. And, unless you are a professional tennis player, your backhand stroke would be your weaker stroke. So, Jesus was not talking about a kill-shot. This is not a savage assault, as should have been obvious as soon as Jesus started talking about slapping, instead of clubbing or beating. A slap on the cheek stings and is humiliating, but it is not a big deal. A backhanded slap is even weaker. I think this may have been Jesus' point; namely, don't make a mountain out of a molehill. Don't escalate a minor offense into a major confrontation. Accordingly, I believe it would be inaccurate and contrary to the will of God to turn this saying into a general prohibition against fighting—or being contentious—in all circumstances.

It is not only important to pay attention to what Jesus says, but also to what He does not say. He could have used any type of confrontation to make His point in this verse, and he deliberately chose a minor assault. Can you imagine Jesus saying, "Fathers, if marauders confront you while working in your fields and kill one of your sons, also offer unto them your other son who is in the barn"? Or, "Fathers, if home-invaders break into your house and rape your wife, also offer unto them your teenage daughter who is hiding in her room"? I can't imagine Him saying that, because just as we should not treat molehills as mountains, we also should not treat mountains as molehills, and murder and rape are mountains. If all of this is accurate, then we cannot use the "turn the other cheek" remark to dissuade us from all kinds of confrontations—especially ones with significant consequences.

Those who live by the sword die by the sword. Another popular verse that is used to dissuade us from confrontation is Matthew 26:52: those who live by the sword die by the sword. On the night Jesus was betrayed, He was praying in the Garden of Gethsemane when men came to arrest Him. "Then the men stepped forward, seized Jesus and arrested him. With that, one of Jesus' companions reached for his sword, drew it out and struck the servant of the high priest, cutting off his ear. 'Put your sword back in its place,' Jesus said to him, 'for all who draw the sword will die by the sword.'" [Matthew 26:50—52] We automatically apply a moral to these words, but is it possible Jesus was speaking statistically? One is more likely to get hurt or sick or killed or blessed during those activities where he spends a great deal of time. Long-haul truckers, who log hundreds of thousands of miles during the course of their careers, are more likely to get injured on the road than those of us who don't spend nearly as much time behind the wheel. Is that because driving is evil? Of course not. Is that because they are bad drivers? Not usually. It is because this is where they spend a great deal of their time, and wherever you spend a great deal of time is where things are most likely to befall you—good or bad. Similarly, if you make a career in the military, you are more likely to be injured or killed on the battlefield than the average civilian.

Let's take this a step further. True, if you make your living with a sword, you are more likely than others to die by the sword; but Jesus never said that this is a bad way to go. We're all going to die. Personally, I'd much rather die by the sword than by rotting away in a hospital bed while some dread disease eats away at my body causing incessant agony for me and my loved ones over the course of months or years.

Some may dismiss these last two points as sophistry, and I admit that they are weak arguments—although not necessarily untrue. What is not weak, however, is context; so, let's put this verse in context. Earlier that same night while still in the upper room where He shared a meal with His disciples, Jesus reminisced about the time He had sent them on a mission "without purse, bag or sandals" and then asked them, "did you lack anything?" "'Nothing,'" they answered." [Luke 22:35] But it was different now, and Jesus wanted His friends to be prepared. He continued, "But now if you have a purse, take it, and also a bag; and if you don't have a sword, sell your cloak and buy one." [Luke 22:36] Were the disciples aghast that the Prince of Peace would direct them to buy swords? Nope. They were quick to point out that they already were prepared. "See, Lord, here are two swords." [Luke 22:38] And was the Prince of Peace aghast that His disciples were armed? Did He respond to this revelation (which He, undoubtedly already knew) by scolding them? Nope. "That's enough!" he replied." Well, if Jesus thought "That's enough!", then He surely must have anticipated a need to use these weapons—which demolishes the argument that we should never resort to the sword. It can be seen, however, as supporting the argument that we should turn to other forms of "contention" before the sword becomes necessary—and that is one of the purposes of politics. So, why would some of our pastors urge us to stay away from politics if it allows us the opportunity to settle differences before the sword becomes necessary?

Prince of Peace. As we have already noted, one of the favorite texts for Christmas cards comes from the Old Testament; namely, Isaiah 9:6-7: "For to us a child is born, to us a son is given, and the government will be on his shoulders. And he will be called

Wonderful Counselor, Mighty God, Everlasting Father, Prince of Peace. Of the greatness of his government and peace there will be no end." Christians see this as pointing to the future arrival of Messiah. "Government", and presumably politics, figures prominently in these verses, showing up twice. The title "Prince of Peace" is also there. Some Christian misleaders spin this into an argument to avoid war—and politics—at all costs. Carl von Clausewitz, renown Prussian general and military philosopher, wrote, "war is a continuation of politics by other means." And so it is inferred that the Prince of Peace, or any other devoted agent of peace, should avoid politics. That seems a strange conclusion. If war does flow from politics, wouldn't it be wise and beneficial for Christians to enter politics in order to steer it away from combative conclusions?

There is another lesson that needs to be taught by the expression "Prince of Peace." In the original Hebrew text, the phrase that is translated as "Prince of Peace" is "Sar Shalom." The word "Sar" has several meanings, including prince, ruler, leader, chief, official, councilor, noble, and vassal. All of these imply an administrative position of leadership or influence. There also are military applications for the word including captain, general, and commander. Although the Hebrew word "shalom" is usually understood to mean "peace", the kind of peace it refers to is not limited to military matters. Shalom is derived from a root word that denotes wholeness, completeness, and wellness. Throughout much of Jewish literature the word is connected with the notion of "shelemut" or perfection. So, when a Jew wishes you "Shalom", he is not saying he hopes you do not have to go to war today. He is wishing you everything that is necessary to perfect your life and make it whole. Accordingly, the Prince of Peace is not necessarily one who ends or avoids war. He is the one who leads us along pathways of perfection, which fits nicely with Jesus' command "Be perfect, therefore, as your heavenly Father is perfect." [Matthew 5:48] The model here is not necessarily someone who avoids war, but rather someone who contributes to wholeness—and that sometimes requires war.

Blessed are the peace-makers. I ended the last section on "Prince of Peace" by writing, "The model here is not necessarily someone who avoids war, but rather someone who contributes to wholeness —and that sometimes requires war." I bet some of our ideological pacifists are bristling at that remark. I bet they also are ready to respond with Jesus' pronouncement recorded in Matthew 5:9, "Blessed are the peace-makers." If Clausewitz was right and "war is a continuation of politics by other means", wouldn't peace-makers want to avoid politics? Not if what Jesus said about "peace-**makers**" is true—and I think all Christians would agree that everything He said is true.

I need to repeat something I wrote a while back. Pay attention to what Jesus did not say as well as to what He did say. Jesus said blessed are the peace-**makers**. He did not say blessed are the peace-**lovers**. There is a critical difference between the two.

In that you are reading this, you likely are looking at a book or electronic tablet of some kind. You may be sitting on a chair inside a building. Did you have to make that book or tablet or chair or building? No. Why? Because they already existed. We only have to "make" things that do not exist. Accordingly, a "peace-maker" exists in a circumstance where there is no peace—otherwise he would not have to make it. Historically, and Biblically, what is the most common way to make peace when it does not exist? War. So, to say "blessed are the peace-makers" is often another way of saying "blessed are the warriors." Peace-lovers, on the other hand, often contribute to the very hostilities they detest. Let's look at just one historical example that illustrates this.

After four horrific years of war, the Paris Peace Conference convened in January of 1919 in Versailles, France, outside Paris. It produced the Treaty of Versailles which officially ended World War I. Among the terms of that treaty was Article 231 which specified that the Germans accept responsibility for the war and the liability to pay financial reparations to the Allies. Germany also was stripped of many territories that had previously belonged to the German Empire and which often had large German populations. The requirement to pay massive reparations ruined the German economy, causing widespread hardship and resentment. The loss of historically German territories, and the subjugation of large numbers of Germans to foreign rule, was a blot upon their national pride and another cause of hardship and resentment. All this created a social, economic, and political environment ripe for the rise of radical groups. One of those was the National Socialist German Workers' Party headed by Adolf Hitler. Hitler and other German radicals enjoyed some measure of success in the early and mid-1920s while conditions were desperate for many Germans. But as those conditions improved, people lost interest in the fanatical extremists. Then came the Great Depression, and the frail German economy crumbled. The masses were, once again, tossed into destitution and the radicals, once again, gained favor. Hitler became Chancellor in 1933. He promised economic recovery and the restitution of German honor by restoring the German Empire. One of his territorial targets was Czechoslovakia, a nation which had never existed before and which contained large numbers of ethnic Germans, especially in an area known as the Sudetenland. In September, 1938, Hitler was on the verge of invading Czechoslovakia. The prime minister of Great Britain at the time was Neville Chamberlain. He was a peace-lover. The horrors of World War I had made a deep and lasting impression on him, and he wanted to avoid another war at all costs. He flew to Munich, Germany, to meet with Hitler. They worked out a deal. Large chunks of Czechoslovakia, including the Sudetenland, would be lopped off and given back to the Third Reich. In exchange, Hitler agreed to not invade the Czech nation. Chamberlain returned to England on September 30, and exited his plane waving a piece of paper later proclaiming, "I believe it is peace for our time." Although Hitler said he had 'No more territorial demands to make in Europe", six months later he invaded the rest of Czechoslovakia, and six months after that, he invaded Poland, which is considered the beginning of World War II in Europe. In retrospect, historians generally agree that Chamberlain's appeasement of Hitler contributed to the Fuehrer's belief that the western nations were weak and that he could confront them and win. Whereas Chamberlain, the peace-lover, believed he had achieved peace in his time, Hitler saw it differently. He later said, "Our enemies are worms. I saw them crawl at Munich."

By the time Winston Churchill became the British prime minister in May, 1940, the war had begun, and his job was to be a peace-maker. How did he pursue that goal? The same way as most other peace-makers—by fighting. Listen to his own words from a speech to the House of Commons on June 4, 1940, upon the conclusion of the successful Dunkirk evacuation. "We shall defend our island, whatever the cost may be, we shall fight on the beaches, we shall fight on the landing grounds, we shall fight in the fields and in the streets, we shall fight in the hills; we shall never surrender." The word "fight" is used four times as Churchill details his plan for making peace.

Peace-lovers frequently incite the bellicose with their abhorrence for conflict, and by doing so, often create the very war they seek to avoid. Peace-makers often have to clean up the mess caused by peace-lovers—and they do it by fighting. Blessed are the peace-makers.

<u>Judge not.</u> In addition to being contentious, politics is often judgmental, and that, too, we are told, is bad. Jesus said as much, right? "Do not judge, or you too will be judged." [Matthew 7:1] This same message is recorded in Luke 6:37. Here again, this understanding of the verse is curious, because there are so many other places in Scripture where judging is commended, not condemned. That should be the first clue that perhaps this simplistic conclusion that judging is bad is not only simplistic, it is wrong. Before we consult with our old friend—context—let's look at a few other examples of good judging.

Next to Jesus, Moses is one of the most prominent characters in the Bible. He, also, is one of the most popular and laudable. In Exodus 18:13 it says that "The next day Moses took his seat to serve as judge for the people, and they stood around him from morning till evening." The seventh book of the Bible is entitled, *Judges*, and documents the deeds of many heroic leaders who were called judges. Even Jesus speaks favorably about judging. In Luke 12:57 He says, "Why don't you judge for yourselves what is right?" Here He is urging people who have differences with one another to judge for themselves what is right and what is wrong. That kind of sounds like politics when it is done correctly, doesn't it? In John 7:24 Jesus says, "Stop judging by mere appearances, but instead judge correctly." Here Jesus tells the people how to judge, not that they shouldn't.

And now, let's circle back to Matthew 7:1 and look at the context of that verse. Jesus had more to say about judging than merely these nine words. Let's see. "Do not judge, or you too will be judged. For in the same way you judge others, you will be judged, and with the measure you use, it will be measured to you. Why do you look at the speck of sawdust in your brother's eye and pay no attention to the plank in your own eye? [Matthew 7:1—3] I would argue here that the key words are not, "Do not judge" but rather, "in the same way you judge others, you will be judged...." As in John 7:24, Jesus is not forbidding others to judge, "but instead [to] judge correctly." And wouldn't it be nice if that rule were applied to politics where hypocrisy is rampant? You see, far from staying out of politics, Christians should enter the field and bring their beliefs with them to help clean things up.

* * *

Christian misleaders have done an enormous injustice to God and His children by urging them to stay out of politics. This is where Satan has done some of his greatest work, and it is where he will continue to work. If we abandon the field, guess who wins.

We agents of righteousness deserve leaders who will live up to that noble calling. They must have a clear understanding of Scripture and must have the courage to stare Satan in the eye and spit. If they cannot do this, then they must relinquish the pulpit and leave the building. Timid church mice belong in the attic, not the pews, and certainly not the pulpit. When it comes to our church leaders, we must demand the roar of the lion and not tolerate the squeak of the mouse. Kneel before God. Rise up for America. Onward Christian soldiers.

Discussion

"Martin Luther once wrote, 'Even the Devil is God's Devil.'" What does that mean?

"Satan doesn't get to dine at the banquet table. He has to make due with the scraps that fall on the floor." What does that mean?

"So, where would Satan look to find more power? Well, where are the greatest concentrations of power on Earth? Capitals, where the politics of a people play out." Do you agree? If this is true, what would you do if you were the Devil, and you were looking for power? Where would you go to influence the affairs of humans?

The author writes, *"you can always expect Satan to be involved in politics. So, what happens if the righteous stay out of politics? Satan wins."* If this is true, what should Christians do to prevent this?

The author believes that Jesus' mission statement is best expressed in 1 John 3:8, "The reason the Son of God appeared was to destroy the devil's work." Can you think of a verse that does a better job of stating Jesus' mission here on Earth?

"Why do they [the Christian 'misleaders'] tell their flocks to stay out of politics? Can you think of a better formula for failure?" Can you?

"Any pastor who is more concerned about losing the freedom to rake in tax-free donations than with standing up to evil needs to resign." Do you agree? Does this describe your pastor?

"Jesus came here precisely because it was dirty. That's where the need was. That's where the job was." Are there any jobs that God might ask you to do that you would refuse? What?

Did you ever think of the Sanhedrin as a political body? Now that you have, does it make it easier to see that Jesus was political?

Regarding Romans 13 and God's admonition to submit to governing authorities, the author writes, *"Not all rulers, administrators, supervisors, officials, etc. are authorities. One is only an authority if one faithfully serves the author, and one is only an authority while one is serving the author. Just being the boss or the mayor or the governor or the president does not make one an authority… If the boss does not serve the author, he or she is not an authority. If a boss used to serve the author but then stops, he or she ceases to be an authority."* Have you ever heard a pastor talk about Romans 13 and include this information? Probably not.

The author argues that, *"When government officials command what God forbids, or forbid what God commands, they are not authorities. We are obligated to obey God—always. We are obligated to disobey the ungodly always—even violently if necessary."* Would you agree? Weren't there Old Testament heroes who fought against evil leaders? Name some.

"To sum up, only those officials who faithfully obey the "author" are "authorities", and the ultimate author is God." Is that clear enough for you?

Jesus said, *"If anyone slaps you on the right cheek, turn to them the other cheek also."* [Matthew 5:39] Do you think this means that we should never fight back against people who attack us? If so, how do you reconcile that belief with all the times God orders His people to fight against their, and His, enemies?

Jesus said, "for all who draw the sword will die by the sword." Many argue that we should never "draw the sword." Re-read how the author responded to this argument. Do you believe there are ever just times to "draw the sword"? Give some examples.

The author argues that one of the nobler purposes of politics is to resolve disputes peacefully before they become violent. If that is so, then how wise is it for pastors and other church leaders to urge parishioners to avoid politics? As the author notes in the next section on the "Prince of Peace", *"If war does flow from politics, wouldn't it be wise and beneficial for Christians to enter politics in order to steer it away from combative conclusions?"* Should you point this out to pastors who argue we should avoid politics?

The author points out that the term "Prince of Peace" is translated from the Hebrew expression, "Sar Shalom", and that the word "Shalom" is related to the word "shelemut" which refers to completeness and perfection. So, the Prince of Peace is not limited to merely avoiding war and violence. He is committed to accomplishing personal and social perfection and wholeness. Are these objectives that occasionally require fighting? If you don't believe so, then how do you reconcile your belief with all the God-directed violence in the Old Testament?

The author draws a distinction between the terms "peace-makers" and "peace-lovers." Jesus referred to "peace-makers", and, as the author notes, "We only have to 'make' things that do not exist." Do you think it is possible that Jesus, in referring to "peace-makers", is talking about those who live where there is no peace and find themselves in a position to have to create it? Do you agree with the author that historically and Biblically one of the most common ways to make peace is through war? Therefore, is it occasionally correct to argue that "to say 'blessed are the peace-makers' is often another way of saying 'blessed are the warriors'"?

The author used the example of the British Prime Minister Neville Chamberlain to argue that "Peace-lovers…often contribute to the very hostilities they detest." Do you agree with him?

Politics is often judgmental, and Jesus said "Do not judge…." But, as the author points out, Jesus said more than that: "in the same way you judge others, you will be judged…." This led the author to argue, *that the key words are not, 'Do not judge' but rather, 'in the same way you judge others, you will be judged….'"* It seems that Jesus' point was not that we should never judge, but rather, that we should always judge carefully and correctly. The author then asks, *"And wouldn't it be nice if that rule were applied to politics where hypocrisy is rampant?"* Christians have a lot to offer politics. Why would we want to withhold that?

The author argues that it is through politics that *"Satan has done some of his greatest work, and it is where he will continue to work."* If Christians fail to show up on that battlefield, can we hold out any hope for righteousness in society?

The author argues that our pastors and church leaders must boldly face Satan wherever he appears—including politics. He writes, *"Timid church mice belong in the attic, not the pews, and certainly not the pulpit. When it comes to our church leaders, we must demand the roar of the lion and not tolerate the squeak of the mouse."* Does your pastor roar or squeak?

PART THREE:

Redemption

"If my people, who are called by my name, will humble themselves and pray and seek my face and turn from their wicked ways, then I will hear from heaven, and I will forgive their sin and will heal their land."

2 Chronicles 7:14

CHAPTER TWELVE:

Going Home

This continent was discovered by a man who sought to "bring the Word of God to unknown coastlands." The "principal effect" to be accomplished by many of those who first established British colonies in the New World was "the conversion…of the people in those parts unto the true worship of God and Christian religion." The first schools established by these devout settlers were intended to further the quest for "Truth for Christ and the Church" among their students. The Revolution was fought by people of faith who honored "the Laws of Nature and of Nature's God" to guarantee the "unalienable Rights" that had been "endowed by their Creator" while "appealing to the Supreme Judge of the world for the rectitude of our intentions". The victors of that War for Independence wrote a Constitution that was "ordained" "to form a more perfect Union" and which acknowledged Jesus to be "our Lord." The first president of that "more perfect Union" declared "that the propitious smiles of Heaven can never be expected on a nation that disregards the eternal rules of order and right which Heaven itself has ordained…." The first Congress of that Union hired two pastors to pray over the legislature and passed a Thanksgiving resolution calling for "a day of public thanksgiving and prayer to be observed by acknowledging, with grateful hearts, the many signal favors of Almighty God, especially by affording them an opportunity peaceably to establish a Constitution of government for their safety and happiness." The president who wrote and issued that Thanksgiving Proclamation said that "it is the duty of all Nations to acknowledge the providence of Almighty God, to obey his will, to be grateful for his benefits, and humbly to implore his protection and favor…." The second president of that nation believed "Our Constitution was made only for a moral and religious people." The third president of that nation ordered that the Bible be used as a reader in the Washington, D.C. public schools. More than a century later, a Supreme Court opinion declared "this is a Christian nation." More than a century after that ruling, this message has been lost to most Americans, and the consequences have been devastating.

We have abandoned the God who protected, preserved, and prospered us. This unfathomable foolishness has cost us dearly, and some wonder if there is any hope for redemption. Many have retreated into a theological cave, bricked up the opening, and decided to pin their hopes for avoiding catastrophe on the Rapture. Is our situation hopeless? Surely, we do not deserve rescue; but we serve a God who is famous for not afflicting sinners with what they do deserve while lavishing them with blessings they do not deserve. Is there any reason to believe that we could be so blessed?

Yes.

Jesus told a beautiful story about a father's love that is recorded in the fifteenth chapter of *Luke*. It is a story every parent can understand. Our children may disappoint, disobey, and even abandon us, but they never stop being our children, and we never stop loving them and hoping for reconciliation. Here's the way Jesus told it.

> "There was a man who had two sons. The younger one said to his father, 'Father, give me my share of the estate.' So he divided his property between them. Not long after that, the younger son got together all he had, set off for a distant country and there squandered his wealth in wild living. After he had spent everything, there was a severe famine in that whole country, and he began to be in need. So he went and hired himself out to a citizen of that country, who sent him to his fields to feed pigs. He longed to fill his stomach with the pods that the pigs were eating, but no one gave him anything. When he came to his senses, he said, 'How many of my father's hired servants have food to spare, and here I am starving to death! I will set out and go back to my father and say to him: Father, I have sinned against heaven and against you. I am no longer worthy to be called your son; make me like one of your hired servants.' So he got up and went to his father. But while he was still a long way off, his father saw him and was filled with compassion for him; he ran to his son, threw his arms around him and kissed him. The son said to him, 'Father, I have sinned against heaven and against you. I am no longer worthy to be called your son.' But the father said to his servants, 'Quick! Bring the best robe and put it on him. Put a ring on his finger

and sandals on his feet. Bring the fattened calf and kill it. Let's have a feast and celebrate. For this son of mine was dead and is alive again; he was lost and is found.' So they began to celebrate." [Luke 15:11—24]

The love of the father in this story was so great that he could look past the past and embrace a new and loving future that he, himself, would create. Our Heavenly Father's love is even greater. He, too, can look past the past; and, although He cannot dismiss our sins as though they never happened and ignore the consequences of iniquity, He can forgive and even pay the price of our rebellion in order to forge a righteous, joyous, and loving future with us. He opens the door so we can come home. He offers each individual that option. History teaches that He will do the same for repentant nations.

In Chapter Ten of this book, we took a brief look at what happened to the Northern Kingdom of Israel (also known as Samaria) and the Southern Kingdom of Judah after they habitually ignored God and pursued other idols. It wasn't good. It also wasn't over. God's indictment was clear and His retribution was brutal, but He also looked forward to a new, refreshed relationship with the Jews of Israel and Judah. Do we have any reason to believe that He would not do the same for the Americans of the United States? Let's look at God's own words to see what can be in store for us.

The thirty-second chapter of Jeremiah contains God's indictment against Judah and the sentence He imposed.

"Therefore this is what the Lord says: I am about to give this city into the hands of the Babylonians and to Nebuchadnezzar king of Babylon, who will capture it. The Babylonians who are attacking this city will come in and set it on fire; they will burn it down, along with the houses where the people aroused my anger by burning incense on the roofs to Baal and by pouring out drink offerings to other gods." [Jeremiah 32: 28—29]

That was God's short-term plan, but the Eternal One always has a longer vision as well. This same chapter also records what God will do next.

"this is what the Lord, the God of Israel, says: 'I will surely gather them from all the lands where I banish them in my furious anger and great wrath; I will bring them back to this place and let them live in safety. They will be my people, and I will be their God. I will give them singleness of heart and action, so that they will always fear me and that all will then go well for them and for their children after them. I will make an everlasting covenant with them: I will never stop doing good to them, and I will inspire them to fear me, so that they will never turn away from me. I will rejoice in doing them good and will assuredly plant them in this land with all my heart and soul.' This is what the Lord says: 'As I have brought all this great calamity on this people, so I will give them all the prosperity I have promised them. [Jeremiah 32:35—42]

Despite their iniquity and offenses against God, He promises to "bring them back", "let them live in safety", and cause "all...[to] go well for them and for their children." He will bring His children home. He "will make an everlasting covenant with them" and "never stop doing good to them." In fact, He "will rejoice in doing them good" and "will give them all the prosperity [He has] promised them."

What does this tell us about our God? His long game is always love. The righteous God must punish sin. The loving Father must bless His children. We can count on both these things. In the end, God will bless us, but why wait until the end. Why not start now?

How do we accomplish this? God told us clearly what we need to do. "If my people, who are called by my name, will humble themselves and pray and seek my face and turn from their wicked ways, then I will hear from heaven, and I will forgive their sin and will heal their land." [2 Chronicles 7:14] Those words were originally spoken to the people of Israel, but they apply just as clearly to us. Notice the four things we need to do to go home. Humble ourselves. Pray. Seek God's face. Turn from our wicked ways. All of these must be more than merely words we say. They must be things we do.

Humble ourselves.

To humble oneself requires that we acknowledge God as Lord and to obey Him faithfully and consistently. As "Lord" we recognize His absolute, unquestioned, and eternal sovereignty. He, and He alone, is the boss, and accepting Him as such is something we must live, not just say.

Humility is not something that comes easily for many of us—and with good reason. Humility requires that we submit to others, and when dealing with selfish humans, that often doesn't work out very well for us. Others will use their power over us to advance themselves, often to our disadvantage. But that is not God's way. He wants you to follow Him because He can give you far more than anyone else ever can. Embedded in the passage above from Jeremiah is this verse: "I will give them singleness of heart and action, so that they will always fear me and that all will then go well for them and for their children after them." [Jeremiah 32:39] The word "fear" in this verse is misleading. God wants us to respect Him and acknowledge His power, but He doesn't want us to live in terror of Him. Elsewhere, this word is translated as "worship", and that may provide a better way to understand this verse. By humbling ourselves before God, we connect and cooperate with Him, and "all will then go well for [us] and for [our] children." As it says in James 4:10, "Humble yourselves before the Lord, and He will lift you up." God doesn't want to oppress you. He wants to bless you. God doesn't want to grind you into the earth. He wants to lift you up to Heaven. Let Him take the reins.

Pray.

Prayer, simply, is talking **with** God—not talking **to** God, which is what most of us do. Prayer needs to be a two-way conversation. Tell Him what's on your mind and in your heart, but then listen to what He has to say. Many of us pay, sometimes dearly, to get the advice of experts. Would it make any sense to ignore what they have to say? Of course not. Well, in God we have access to advice from the greatest Expert of all—and He doesn't even charge us. Does it make any sense to ignore what He has to say? OF COURSE NOT! And then, when you get the advice, follow it.

This next step is critical. Once you say the prayer, become the prayer. I've found that this is one of the best ways to see your prayers answered the way you hope they will. What does it mean to "become the prayer"? Become a part of God's plan to answer your prayer. For example, if you pray for God to help an elderly friend in need, after completing your prayer hurry to that friend to provide the help he needs. Once you pray for a loved-one's healing, go visit him. If you have a heart for the addicted or the depressed or the homeless, ask God to help them, then go do exactly what you asked God to do. Don't expect God to answer your prayers unless you prove to Him that this means enough to you to become the answer yourself.

Seek His face.

When you are having a meaningful, in-person conversation with someone, where are you likely looking? Probably at his or her face, and especially the eyes. A great deal of communication is non-verbal and best perceived by looking at facial expressions. It has been said that the eyes are the windows to the soul, so this is where we gaze when we are truly intent on understanding the message of another—or with conveying our message to him. Allowing your gaze to drift off elsewhere breaks the connection. It suggests a loss of interest or a casualness about the topic of the conversation or about the person with whom you are talking. The Hebrew word for "face" in the Old Testament is sometimes translated as "presence." If both parties to a conversation are not present—both physically and in terms of one's attention—then the purpose of the conversation will not likely be accomplished. Every parent knows this, which is why they often demand that a child "look at me when I'm talking to you." Right? Without that face-to-face connection, the listener will likely get distracted and miss the point of the conversation. So, when God says to "seek my face", in essence He is repeating the admonition of most other good parents; namely, "look to me when I'm talking to you."

Although we cannot see God's face in the same way we can see the visage of others around us, we can choose to intently connect with Him and pay attention to all that He is communicating. This is what it means to "seek His face." We connect with His presence, seek His character, and look for His truth so that we may better understand and obey.

Turn from your wicked ways.

"Turn from your wicked ways" is another way of saying "Repent." The Hebrew word that is translated as "repent" is "shuv", and it means to go a different direction. The Greek word that is often translated as "repent" is "metanoiein", and it generally means to change one's mindset. So, if we truly want to accomplish the healing of our land that is promised in 2 Chronicles 7:14, it is not enough to simply demonstrate humility, talk with God, and earnestly seek His presence and wisdom. We have to change. We have to "go a different direction" and change our "mindset." We must stop all the ungodly practices we have adopted and "seek first his kingdom and his righteousness." [Matthew 6:33]

Jesus told another parable about a another farmer who also had two sons.

"There was a man who had two sons. He went to the first and said, 'Son, go and work today in the vineyard.' 'I will not,' he answered, but later he changed his mind and went. Then the father went to the other son and said the same thing. He answered, 'I will, sir,' but he did not go. Which of the two did what his father wanted?" [Matthew 21:28—31]

The answer, of course, was the first son. God is not looking for lip-service. He is looking for obedience, and even though the first son in this story started off in the wrong direction, he eventually changed his mind and got it right. This is exactly what we in the United States also need to do. No more lip-service. No more "God bless America." It is time for America to bless God.

Discussion

"We have abandoned the God who protected, preserved, and prospered us. This unfathomable foolishness has cost us dearly...." List some ways that abandoning God has hurt us as a nation.

"[God's] long game is always love. The righteous God must punish sin. The loving Father must bless His children. We can count on both these things." If the righteous God must punish sin, what do you think this will mean for America? If the loving Father must bless His children, what do you think this will mean for America?

In 2 Chronicles 7:14, God says He will forgive the sins of a nation and heal the land if its people "will humble themselves and pray and seek my face and turn from their wicked ways...." Consider each of these four conditions.

What does it mean for Americans to "humble themselves"?

How should we pray?

What does it mean to "seek [God's] face"?

What specifically do we need to do to turn from our wicked ways?

The author writes, *"Don't expect God to answer your prayers unless you prove to Him that this means enough to you to become the answer yourself."* Do you treat prayer as mere lip service? Do you think you have done enough for others if you just ask God to help them but are unwilling to do anything yourself? What do you think it means to "become the prayer"?

The author says that turning from our wicked ways requires that *"We have to 'go a different direction' and change our 'mindset.'"* Are you willing to make the effort to do this? What would this mean for Americans?

Which request is more likely to get results, to ask that God bless America, or to ask that America blesses God?

CHAPTER THIRTEEN:

The Fault with the Default

I remember a political cartoon from many years ago. It depicted a prominent politician as a young child standing in front of a chalkboard in his classroom. On the board the teacher had written many questions of various types. 2 + 2=____. The first president of the United States was____. The process plants use to make their own food is called____. How many planets are in our Solar System?____ The schoolboy had written the same answer for every question: "government."

"Government" has become the default answer for all our problems. There are poor people. What's the government going to do about it? There are people without healthcare. What's the government going to do about it? There is a new virus that threatens to become a pandemic. What's the government going to do about it? I have a hangnail. What's the government going to do about it?

This reliance on government is problematic for many reasons. In Chapter Six I wrote that nearly all governments throughout history have been feudal kleptocracies. Feudal kleptocrats (the power elite) love big government because that is the machine they use to steal from the people and preserve their own power. The bigger the government, the more powerful the elite, and the more able they are to fleece the populace. The Founders and Framers understood this, which is why they sought to limit the size of government—drastically. They understood the necessary connection between big government and little liberties. Here's a quick course on why this is true. Governments operate by making, administering, and adjudicating laws. Laws, by there very nature, almost always work to limit freedoms. Think about it. We don't need laws to make people do things they are naturally going to do. As essential as is breathing, I doubt there is a law anywhere on Earth which regulates it. People are going to breathe. We also don't need laws to keep people from doing things they naturally won't do. I doubt there is a law anywhere on Earth forbidding people from bathing in sulphuric acid. Nobody is going to do that. We only need laws to make people do things they otherwise wouldn't, or to prevent them from doing things they otherwise would. And all of this limits individual liberties. Some of this is necessary. Anytime two or more people choose to collaborate and live or work together, there needs to be some rules, and some compromises must be made. But the more rules there are, the more compromises will be imposed— usually upon the weaker party—and so, "compromise" generally amounts to abuse. When it comes to government, the more laws there are, the bigger the government becomes, and the smaller becomes the range of personal freedoms; and that only benefits the power elite.

There is a quote that has been attributed to Thomas Jefferson. He likely didn't say or write it, but it is a sage warning all the same. "A government big enough to give you everything you want, is a government big enough to take away everything that you have."

Another problem with relying on the government to deal with all our problems and ambitions is that it rarely does a good job. During various speaking events, I have occasionally offered the following challenge to my audiences: Name five things that the federal government does well. By "well" I mean effectively and efficiently. "Effectively" means the intended goals are accomplished. "Efficiently" means the intended goals are accomplished with a minimum of cost and waste. I've only ever had two answers. The one I usually get is the military. My response is that our military is the best in the world (or, at least, it was until very recently) but I don't think the Department of Defense is going to receive any awards for efficiency. They're the ones who make the $400 hammers and the $600 toilet seats. The other answer— offered only once—was the cross-country railroad. I confessed that I was not expert on the subject, although I seemed to recall some cases of graft and corruption associated with the project. I then asked the person who offered that answer if he could think of any example that took place in the last 100 years. His eyes rolled upward—apparently gazing at the same thing as everyone else in the room—and he remained silent. My point was this: If we can't even think of five things, three things, or one thing that the federal government does well, why would we want to keep entrusting more and more areas of our lives to it?

There also is what we might call the "Slime Factor" associated with relying on politicians to solve our problems and pursue our dreams. Sadly, these often are not people of high moral character.

We've had several presidents in recent decades guilty of adultery—even serial adultery—sexual abuse, abusing their power for personal gain, illegal business dealings, and coercion to name a few. And these sins are not limited to those who have worked from the Oval Office. These offenses, along with many others including perjury, lies, hypocrisy, and a rich variety of other forms of corruption, are commonplace among our political leaders. And a telling fact is that the reader cannot deduce that I must be either a Republican or a Democrat because everybody knows that these claims apply to members of your own team, regardless of which team that is. Is this really a very good pool of talent to draw from, especially when we are seeking a moral reformation? So, is our goal of redemption hopeless? Not at all, especially once you break out of the mindset that our efforts must be political in nature. Remember, "government" is not the answer to every problem. In fact, it is a poor answer to most problems, and that suggests that politicians will often fail to provide true solutions to our challenges. Let's look at a real issue that hangs like a storm cloud over us all and which demonstrates how politicians—blinded by the obsession to increase their power—can fail to provide effective solutions.

Dealing with "gun violence" has become a cause celebre for many politicians and certain political organizations. As I am writing this, news outlets are busy covering yet another case of an adolescent with a firearm causing multiple deaths at a public school. It seems like something similar to this happens every few weeks; and yet, when I was young, you never heard of it. Perhaps the first modern event in this class of violence took place on August 1, 1966. Charles Whitman, a student at the University of Texas at Austin, killed his mother and then his wife before heading to the clock tower at the university. After hauling up various weapons and several hundred rounds of ammunition, he first killed the receptionist on the 28th floor of the building. Next, he gunned down a family of tourists who were preparing to enter the reception area. Two died and two others were seriously wounded. Whitman then occupied his sniper nests overlooking the campus in all directions. From 11:48 a.m. until 1:24 p.m., the gunman fired approximately 150 rounds, killing 14 and wounding 31 others, one of whom died years later from complications resulting from the wounds. His murderous rampage finally ended when three Austin police patrol officers and an armed citizen ambushed and killed Whitman. The news was received with shock. This was unheard of.

Now, news of another mass shooting is received with reactions like, "Not again."

Enter the politicians. Mass shootings like this have become fodder in the debate about the Second Amendment and restricting weapon ownership. The reasoning on the anti-gun side seems to be that if we take away the guns, gun violence will end. Well, maybe "gun" violence would end, but violence would not. Violence does not happen because of what we hold in our hands; but rather, because of what we hold in our hearts. As long as we regard our brothers and sisters as deplorable reprobates and villains, or as valueless clumps of cells, violence will continue—if not with guns, then with knives. If not with knives, then with bats. If not with bats, then with sticks. If not with sticks, then with rocks. If not with rocks then with fists and feet and teeth. But notice, the politicians do not deal with the root cause of gun violence (which is the interpersonal animosity they often have helped to create). They seek political gain, which, in the case of the anti-gun gangs (which almost always happen to be the big-government gangs), is to further emaciate the people by removing their last defense against the abuses of government and tyrannical politicians. The real purpose of the Second Amendment was not to indulge sportsmen, nor to allow hunters to feed their families, nor even to empower individuals to protect themselves from violent criminals. The real purpose of the Second Amendment was to allow the people to protect themselves from the worst abusers of civil liberties and the worst mass-murders of all time; namely, governments and the people who run them. Since violence is the ultimate arbiter, anyone who is denied access to violence as a defense will always be vulnerable to those who have access to violence. Taking away people's guns won't end gun violence. It will simply limit the perpetration of gun violence to those who still have the guns, which would be the criminals, the government, and its agents.

The real solution to this violence is not political. It is spiritual. Charles Whitman was raised by a brutal man who abused him and his mother. Had Whitman's father been a devout, practicing Christian, the "Texas Clocktower" would never had entered the lexicon of American crime stories. The solutions to most of our problems are not political. They are spiritual. We need to shift our focus heavenward if we truly want to improve things here on Earth.

2 Chronicles 7:14 tells us what we must do. How do we do this? Who is best qualified to accomplish this? This takes us back to the American philosophy of government we discussed in Chapter Six: "Governments are instituted among men to secure these rights that are endowed by their Creator." If the rightful role of government is to do the work of God, doesn't it make sense that the best people to accomplish this are the people of God—the church not the political parties—the believers not the politicians?

I wrote in the last chapter that the Greek word that is often translated as "repent" is "metanoiein", and it generally means to change one's mindset. This is precisely what we must do. We must free ourselves from the mindset that the government is the only, or the best, or even a good means for solving our problems. It is not. We must destroy the mindset that it is the politicians who will save us. They will not. We must escape the trap that leads us to trust the Democratic or the Republican National Corporations to provide the guidance we need to rebuild America the good, the great, and the Godly. The last several decades should have convinced us that these national parties are committed only to their own power interests and that we the people are merely "useful idiots" to be exploited for their political gains. Well, if we cannot trust the elephant or the donkey, whom can we trust?

The Lion and the Lamb.

God has never failed us, and He never will. History—indeed eternity—proves that without God, you cannot win. With God, you cannot lose. So, why not go with God—or rather, why not go back to God? It worked before, and it will work again.

Mark Twain (Samuel Clemens) is not usually remembered as a devout Christian. Indeed, his religious beliefs seemed to transition throughout his life. A Protestant in his youth, he dabbled in Deism for a while and then crab-walked back to some form of skeptical relationship with the Bible and its claims. However he may have ended his Earthly journey, there were times when he did not accept the existence of Heaven nor Hell and questioned the immortality of the soul as well as the divinity of Jesus. He recorded in his "Notebook", "If Christ were here, there is one thing he would not be—a Christian." Why? Twain was a clear-eyed student of Christian history and wrote in his autobiography, "There is one notable thing about our Christianity: bad, bloody, merciless, money-grabbing and predatory...ours is a terrible religion." No honest observer can deny that the practice of Christians has often failed to live up to the aspirations of our Christ. But that doesn't mean that we shouldn't keep trying, and Twain seemed to believe this as well.

In a magazine interview less than five years before his death, Twain said,

"I will be conceded ... that a Christian's first duty is to God. It then follows, as a matter of course, that it is his duty to carry his Christian code of morals to the polls and vote them. If Christians should vote their duty to God at the polls, they would carry every election and do it with ease.... If the Christians of America could be persuaded to vote God and a clean ticket, it would bring about a moral revolution that would be incalculably beneficent. It would save the country." September 2, 1905

Here, in a nutshell, is the overview of what we need to do to save America. If Christians registered to vote (which they often do not), studied their Bibles (which they rarely do), kept informed about current events (again, not a strong suit of ours), and voted the Bible, "It would save the country."

So, this is an overview of what we need to do. In the next chapters, we will go into some more details regarding how to do this.

Discussion

Do you agree that *"Laws, by there very nature, almost always work to limit freedoms"*? Other than laws that actually create liberties, like the Constitution, can you name a law that does not limit freedoms?

"When it comes to government, the more laws there are, the bigger the government becomes, and the smaller becomes the range of personal freedoms; and that only benefits the power elite." Do you agree or disagree? State your case.

The author states that he has *"occasionally offered the following challenge to my audiences: Name five things that the federal government does well."* Can you name five things the federal government does well?

"There also is what we might call the 'Slime Factor' associated with relying on politicians to solve our problems and pursue our dreams. Sadly, these often are not people of high moral character." The term "morality" generally refers to principles concerning the distinction between right and wrong as well as defining good and bad behavior. But in most moral systems, right, wrong, good behavior, and bad behavior is expressed in terms of how we treat one another. So, if politicians often possess poor morals, by definition they will be bad at treating people well. Do we really want to entrust these people with protecting and enriching our well-being?

"The real solution to this violence is not political. It is spiritual." Do you agree or disagree? What do you think is the cause of interpersonal violence? How can we limit it?

"We must free ourselves from the mindset that the government is the only, or the best, or even a good means for solving our problems. It is not." If government and politics were good at solving problems, why do we have so many? If we decide not to rely on government so much, upon what should we rely?

"God has never failed us, and He never will. History—indeed eternity—proves that without God, you cannot win. With God, you cannot lose. So, why not go with God—or rather, why not go back

to God? It worked before, and it will work again." Do you agree, and are you willing to give it a chance?

Mark Twain said, "If the Christians of America could be persuaded to vote God and a clean ticket, it would bring about a moral revolution that would be incalculably beneficent. It would save the country." The author believes *"Here, in a nutshell, is the overview of what we need to do to save America. If Christians registered to vote (which they often do not), studied their Bibles (which they rarely do), kept informed about current events (again, not a strong suit of ours), and voted the Bible, 'It would save the country.'"* Do you think the future of America rests with the Democrats, the Republicans, or the Christians? Why?

CHAPTER FOURTEEN:

Time to Crash the Party—

Again

Stephan Pastis is the creator of a comic strip entitle "Pearls Before Swine." The main characters are animals, and their names correspond with their specie—mostly. For example, there is a rat whose name is "Rat", a pig whose name is "Pig", and a goat whose name is "Goat." There are other characters, including a benighted crocodile named "Larry"—thanks for that one, Steph. The episode that ran on October 1, 2024, has a special relevance for the present chapter. Rat is bellowing, "We need to fix everything that's wrong with this country!" Goat replies, "Yeah, I agree, so I sketched out this possible solution to some of our problems." After perusing the plan, Rat responds, "Yeah, this looks like it could work. Does my side win?" Goat answers, "This isn't about what political party wins. It's about solving real problems." Rat looks Goat squarely in the eyes and says, "So you've wasted everyone's time?" Goat doesn't get it. He answers, "What am I missing here?" Rat, fist in the air, comes back, "We want victories, not solutions!" And there, in a nutshell, is the essence of life with political parties. It's not about solutions or what's right or what benefits the nation. Those are just catchphrases and platitudes used to delude the masses. Politics is about power, and you don't get power if you don't win.

In 2013 I published another handbook: *AR2; Handbook for the Second American Revolution* [Cross and Eagle Press]. (In case you didn't get it, "AR2" stands for "American Revolution #2.") Some people become very agitated at the use of the word "revolution." If you are one of them, keep in mind that revolutions do not have to be violent and bloody. In fact, one of the purposes of the *AR2 Handbook* was to offer revolutionary ideas for reforming a decaying America before our only options for the future were death or CW2—the second Civil War, which certainly would be violent and bloody.

Chapter Seven of *AR2* is entitled "Time to Crash the Party; No Party Affiliation." It discussed many problems of the party system in America. All those problems still afflict us. They need to be addressed and this party system needs to be replaced with a Biblical option. I thought I would simply repeat that chapter here to familiarize you with the troubles of the party system and why we need to end it. After that, we can discuss an alternative.

TIME TO CRASH THE PARTY

No Party Affiliation

Millions of Americans have experienced the thrill and terror of starting their own businesses. Frequently the motivation for such an endeavor is to build "a better mousetrap." Someone told Mom that her cookies and cakes were so good that she ought to open a bakery. Someone admires Dad's woodworking skills and urges him to start a carpentry shop. A faithful employee keeps suggesting ways to improve the business to the boss, but the boss keeps brushing him off. Finally, the employee decides to go out on his own and prove himself right. At first the goal of these mom-and-pop startups is quality. The entrepreneur believes he has a better idea and wants to share it with the world. At some point, however, this shining idealism is tarnished, and more mundane objectives take over. "I'm overworked. I have no time for my family. Life has become drudgery. I need to make more money. I must expand my operation." Mom starts using preservatives and less expensive ingredients. Dad starts using screws and nails instead of tongue and groove. The former employee starts acting more and more like his former employer. Compromises are made. Principles are sacrificed. Instead of selling the best, we sell-out to be the best. It becomes about winning, instead of that for which you seek to win. The little shop that made it right abandons its ideals to become the mega-chain that made the most.

This isn't a trait of business. It is a trait of human nature. It manifests itself in manifold areas -- including, and perhaps especially, in politics.

When the sun rose over New York City on the morning of April 30, 1789, it would soon illuminate a remarkable event. The first

President of the United States under the Constitution would be inaugurated. In more ways than one, a new day had dawned.

George Washington had been the only Commander of the Continental Army during the eight years of the Revolution. He accomplished the impossible. He defeated the greatest empire on earth with a ragtag band of ill-trained and poorly-supplied troops. In 1787 Washington was chosen to be the President of the Constitutional Convention. He accomplished the impossible. He oversaw the drafting of a profoundly wise and innovative plan of government that united thirteen proud, diverse, and divisive sovereign states into one grand union. Two years later Washington was unanimously selected by the Electoral College to lead this new nation. He accomplished the impossible. His wisdom and character provided the glue that held the often contradictory and contrary elements of a far-flung country together and gave it a sense of direction, identity, and mission that would propel it to greatness. He was the "indispensable man." It is too bad that modern-day fools have sought to dispense with him.

When George Washington became President, there were no political parties. Washington liked it that way, and he would have preferred that it stayed that way. Unfortunately, it didn't last long. In 1791 the Federalist Party emerged with Alexander Hamilton and John Adams as its leaders. The next year the Anti-Federalist, or Democratic-Republican Party, arose under the leadership of Thomas Jefferson. This was a development that greatly concerned Washington and threatened the unity of his administration. You see, all three of the men cited above were members of Washington's leadership team. Adams was Vice-President, Hamilton was Secretary of the Treasury, and Jefferson was Secretary of State. As the president of a republic, and not the king of a monarchy, Washington could not stop the rise of political parties, but he advised against them as earnestly as he could. In his farewell address, Washington warned of the "disorders and miseries" which could be expected from the development of a party system. He alerted us to the "common and continual mischiefs of the spirit of party...." This party spirit "kindles the animosity of one part against another, foments occasionally riot and insurrection." He sagely advised that it is "the interest and duty of a wise people to discourage and restrain it." Sadly, the indispensable wisdom of the indispensable man was dispensed with.

Washington was not alone in this judgment against parties. Thomas Paine, the pamphleteer of the American Revolution, is perhaps best known for the opening line of The American Crisis: *"These are the times that try men's souls", first published in late 1776. This same luminary of the Great Rebellion also weighed in on the divisiveness of parties. "Let the names of Whig and Tory [the two major political viewpoints of Englishmen at the time] be extinct; and let none other be heard among us, than those of a good citizen, a resolute friend, and a virtuous supporter of the rights of mankind and of the free and independent states of America." More good advice that has been ignored.*

Every modern-American has grown up in a country where the government has been dominated by two political parties. The experience has been so universal that it is hard to imagine it could be anything different. But we must imagine. In fact, we must dare to act and recreate.

Washington was right. The party system simply has caused too many "disorders and miseries." It started out nobly -- perhaps -- but its genetic code is loaded with so many noxious elements that it is virtually impossible for it to grow without developing some terrible deformity or disease. Like the mom-and-pop companies mentioned above, a party often starts off with lofty ideals, but then the "business" of politics takes over, and the goal shifts from doing what is right to doing what will win. The interests of the party -- and especially of those who run the party machine -- take precedence over the interests of the people. The goal isn't to serve the masses. The goal is to hoodwink the masses into supporting "our" side long enough so that the fat cats who run the machine can fleece them. And lest the reader should think that I have gone 'round the bend into the dark shadows of wacky, conspiratorial theorists, consider this. I personally listened to a candidate for state party chairman of one of the "Big Two" parties in one of the biggest states in the Union as he campaigned for votes at a county central committee meeting. Did he speak of lofty ideals or the rectitude of their party's platform? Not one word. What he did talk about was the need to get more money and more votes. His plan for doing this was essentially to become more like the "other guys" because they were doing such a stellar job of humiliating his old, grand party at the polls. Apparently, the strategy is, "If you can't beat 'em, join 'em -- just keep it a secret." By the way, this candidate won election handily.

Let us look at a few of the glaring problems associated with party politics and the party system. First of all, keep in mind that the "Spirit of the Party" is the "Spirit of the Part." Party politics isn't about all of us, it's about some of us. It is divisive, not unifying. It is exclusive, not inclusive. It is adversarial, not amicable. It is institutionalized and legalized warfare, and the battleground is our land, our lives, and our livelihood. It fosters and encourages an "us versus them" attitude. Accordingly, party politics usually devolves into "attack ads" and a laser-like focus on emphasizing differences. A happy, peaceful, and prosperous society, however, requires a healthy measure of unity and agreement. That's just not on the menu of "Party Politics." The party politician needs an enemy and a war. We the people need friends and peace.

In a system where party politics prevail, the party machine becomes the primary path to public office. The party machine is where the action is if you are interested in holding such an office. If you hope to be a successful candidate, you are going to have to get your ticket punched by those who run the machine. Unless you happen to be a celebrity, you will have to pay your dues by serving the party and subordinating your interests to the interests of the party until the party believes you could be useful for accomplishing its purposes. If you do happen to be a celebrity, you can often bypass the party's "time in grade" requirements for being a candidate, but you still will likely be expected to subordinate your interests to those of the machine. Now, remember that in Chapter Two [Chapter two of AR2, not this book] it was pointed out that government concentrates a great deal of power in conveniently compact locations. Accordingly, it was argued that government service "will attract the worst of the worst of us -- the most selfish of the selfish -- like a steaming pile of manure attracts all manner of vile insects." So, if the power of government attracts the worst of us like manure attracts bugs, and if the party machine provides the primary path to government office, I guess that we can conclude that party headquarters is the first steaming pile this side of the capital. As such, party headquarters often functions as a clearing house for scoundrels. Think of all the good that would come if we simply mucked the barn and eliminated these dens of iniquity.

As the pathway to power, the party machines not only attract those who crave that power, they also become lucrative targets of opportunity for those who want to influence the use of that power.

The work of many special interest groups has been made much easier by the party system. Instead of having to confront hundreds of federal legislators and thousands of state law-makers in unending one-to-one encounters, a few well-placed contacts at party headquarters will suffice. The party mechanics will carry the ball for them, and woe be unto any person of conscience who entertains ideas of resistance. Can you spell "One and done"? The party system often opens the door to special interests while slamming it in the face of the general welfare.

Since the party machine paves the pathway to power, the party machine, itself, becomes an organism of unspeakable power. You want power? Pay homage to the Machine. You want to influence the use of that power? Pay the Machine. This accumulation of political and economic might not only gives the party machines power over who may run for office, who will retain office, and who gets to influence those in office; it also gives the machines power over us because they -- not we -- decide who will be our "representatives." They also dictate the agenda that will be pursued. We the people are left to wonder about and wait for the candidates and causes which the Machine decides are best for us.

Certain grass-roots groups have arisen to counter the power of the Machines. A prominent one that surged into the spotlight around 2008 sought to capture and reform the Republican Party. Nice thought. Bad plan. They met with some initial success, but have been fading recently. Why? Like I said, "Nice thought. Bad plan." It is crucial that grass-roots groups arise, but not so they can become "them." They should and must be the antithesis of party politics, not the next stage in its evolution. I'm sure that many grass-rooters thought, "Why reinvent the wheel? Let's just take over the party that seems closest to our ideals." There is some superficial appeal to this idea; unless, of course, the wheel is square. In that case, it might be far more productive to start over from scratch than to attempt to repair the broken wheel. Additionally, the grass-rooters have proved to be no match for the machinations of the veteran party machinists. These machinists are too good at what they do. They will always beat you if you play their game. So, don't play their game. Leave the stadium, find a sandlot somewhere, and play a game that is more interesting to we the people.

Another problem with a system of party politics is that it is a great facilitator of voter fraud -- which has become rampant in modern

America. I volunteered to assist a non-partisan organization which works to minimize voter fraud. Among other things, I received training to assist the county office which maintains the records of eligible voters. I, and others, were trained to look for instances where a voter might be registered more than once -- whether by accident or design. We were taught to flag such entries as "John Doe, born 1/13/85" and "John L. Doe, born 1/13/85" where both lived at the same address. Such multiple entries could allow one person to cast more than one vote. This is especially likely in "vote by mail" which is becoming more prevalent. Frankly, I wondered if I would be able to find any suspected culprits. I was shocked to see that, by the time I finished processing my first stack of records, nearly one-third of the entries were "suspicious." That creates a huge potential for voter fraud; but the ability to turn that potential into a reality is maximized in a party system where a structure exists to organize the fraud and profit from it.

Significant voter fraud is unlikely to develop apart from a system that has longevity -- and parties, like vampires, live a long time. Suppose we had no parties, and each candidate ran on his personal merits. Even if a candidate were inclined to benefit from voter fraud, he would have to invest in a long-term, expensive, illegal, and dangerous effort to amass enough fraudulent votes to sway an election. Should he actually accomplish this, either time or the voters would likely have caught up with him, and he would either retire to the farm or buy one. Parties, however, live long enough to make systematic fraud productive and worth the risk. "Candidate A" may retire or die, but "Candidate B" from the same party will be waiting in the wings. Neither will have the time to build his own cadre of fraudulent voters, but both will be able to cash in on the on-going efforts of the party.

Another dysfunctional aspect of party politics is the tendency to devolve into Pavlovian responses to political proposals. Ivan Pavlov was a Russian physiologist who did a great deal of research on the reflex systems of the body. In what was perhaps his best known experiment, Pavlov would ring a bell before feeding his dogs. Eventually, the dogs associated the ringing of the bell with being fed, and they would actually start to salivate before the food arrived. Similarly, many modern politicians react reflexively to who is proposing or perpetrating a course of action. They are more concerned with the party affiliation of the author of some proposal than with the merits of the proposition. For example, if a

Republican president (Bush) engages in massive deficit spending, Republicans argue that it is reasonable while Democrats find it irresponsible. If a Democratic president (Obama) engages in massive deficit spending, Democrats argue that it is reasonable while Republicans find it irresponsible. Good dog! Now, wipe your chin. In such a system, the merits of a plan often have little to do with the acceptability of a plan. The overriding issue is, "Who will get the credit and how many donations and votes can we garner?" Promoting the general welfare often has little to do with political strategizing between the parties. Politics becomes a sectarian chess match where each side drools over the prospect of ravaging the other side's queen. The political system degenerates into unending head-butting where the politicians get the publicity (along with the payroll, perks, and pensions) while we the people get the migraines. The time has come for we the people to send these slobbering hounds to the kennel and lock them up until they know how to behave in civil society.

So, what is the alternative? No party affiliation -- or better yet, no parties at all.

"My goodness!", the reader may be thinking. "How could that possibly work?" It's easier than you think, and the only reason it doesn't seem simple is because we, like Pavlov's dogs and party politicians, have been conditioned to think in terms of party politics. We have been trained to think and act "inside boxes" that were created by others in order to control our thoughts and actions. Such boxes, however, are no places for a free people, and it is high time for us to bust out of them.

The simple fact is, we don't need parties. Suppose we outlawed the use of such words as "Democrat," "Republican," "right," "left," "liberal," "conservative," or any other descriptive group title. What would candidates talk about? They would talk about the values and principles they believe in and what they would do if elected. Good! That's exactly what they should be talking about and exactly how we voters should be making our decisions. Every campaign would be a grass-roots campaign that focuses on issues, principles, and actions instead of a party moniker.

The reader may be thinking, "Well, that might work at the local level, but you need an organization to carry out a campaign at the state and national level." Do we? I would suggest that you are still a "box-dweller" and need to free your mind. Think about this. Our greatest leaders emerged during a time in our history when political parties did not exist or were in their infancy. George Washington, John Adams, Thomas Jefferson, Benjamin Franklin, Alexander Hamilton, John Hancock, Patrick Henry, Samuel Adams, George Mason, John Jay, James Madison, etc., all rose to prominence and power without the aid of radio, television, the social media, celebrity endorsements, and with precious little -- or no -- help from party machines. I suspect it is no coincidence that the Golden Age of American Statesmen corresponds with a time when political parties were absent or at their weakest. In the absence of party machines, the cream will rise to the top. In a system dominated by party politics, the crumbs will rise to the top.

Discussion

Do you agree that *"Politics is about power, and you don't get power if you don't win"*? If you do agree, then where do moral considerations fit in the world of politics? Would you expect politicians to pursue righteousness if it meant their party would lose? If you don't think politics is about power, then what is it about?

"In his farewell address, Washington warned of the 'disorders and miseries' which could be expected from the development of a party system." List some of the "disorders and miseries" you see in the operation of the party system. Are these "necessary evils", or is there a way to do without the party system?

The author wrote, *"The goal [of the big party machines] isn't to serve the masses. The goal is to hoodwink the masses into supporting 'our' side long enough so that the fat cats who run the machine can fleece them."* Do you agree? Can you give examples of how parties sacrifice the interests of the masses to preserve their own power at the expense of the masses? (Hint: Who benefits from deficit spending, inflation, higher taxes, central banking policies, government regulations of business, government subsidies, etc.?)

The author wrote that the "'Spirit of the Party' is the 'Spirit of the Part.'" Can you see how this is true? What does this mean for us as a nation? Can we be a united people if the parties dominate politics?

Do you agree that party politics "fosters and encourages an 'us versus them' attitude"? What will this do to national harmony?

The author argued that the most selfish of the selfish are attracted to politics for personal reasons. In a party system, these scoundrels usually have to receive the aid and support of the political parties in order to achieve their goals. Accordingly, "party headquarters often functions as a clearing house for scoundrels." Does this sound correct to you? If so, what does this mean for the nation?

Explain why *"The work of many special interest groups has been made much easier by the party system."*

Do you agree that *"The party system often opens the door to special interests while slamming it in the face of the general welfare"*? Explain.

Have you seen that *"We the people are left to wonder about and wait for the candidates and causes which the Machine decides are best for us"*? In the 2024 presidential election, the candidate for one of the major parties never won a primary. So, who chose her to be the candidate?

The author wrote *"It is crucial that grass-roots groups arise, but not so they can become 'them.' They should and must be the antithesis of party politics, not the next stage in its evolution."* Do you agree? Why is it important for grass-roots groups to arise?

Why is it that *"a system of party politics…is a great facilitator of voter fraud"*?

The author wrote that *"Parties, however, live long enough to make systematic [voter] fraud productive and worth the risk."* Explain how that happens.

The author points out that *"many modern politicians react reflexively to who is proposing or perpetrating a course of action. They are more concerned with the party affiliation of the author of some proposal than with the merits of the proposition."* As a result, *"Promoting the general welfare often has little to do with political strategizing between the parties."* Give some examples of this.

"Suppose we outlawed the use of such words as 'Democrat,' 'Republican,' 'right,' 'left,' 'liberal,' 'conservative,' or any other descriptive group title. What would candidates talk about? They would talk about the values and principles they believe in and what they would do if elected. Good! That's exactly what they should be talking about and exactly how we voters should be making our decisions. Every campaign would be a grass-roots campaign that focuses on issues, principles, and actions instead of a party moniker." Can you imagine that working? What problems could arise from such a system?

The author points out that *"it is no coincidence that the Golden Age of American Statesmen corresponds with a time when political parties were absent or at their weakest."* Why is that true?

"In the absence of party machines, the cream will rise to the top. In a system dominated by party politics, the crumbs will rise to the top." Is that true, or just a clever expression?

CHAPTER FIFTEEN:

Serve Him Only

There is another, deeper problem with the political system than just the interplay of parties. Actually, I should say there is another, deeper problem with **a** political system. Politics is all about power —its acquisition, its distribution, and its use. In such a system, winning is the ultimate objective, as Rat clearly understood. In such a system, righteousness is often not an objective at all. At best, it is a slogan. In fact, it usually is an obstacle to the objective; and that should be a problem for all Bible-believing people of faith.

After His baptism, Jesus went into the wilderness for forty days. Near the end of that time, His archenemy, Satan, approached Him and began to tempt Jesus. (Notice, the Vile One generally shows up when we are at our weakest.) He knew why Jesus had come to Earth. He had come to rescue the fallen children of God and to establish the Father's Kingdom "on earth as it is in heaven." Jesus would have to pay a dear price to accomplish that. Satan offered Him an easier way. "Again, the devil took him to a very high mountain and showed him all the kingdoms of the world and their splendor. 'All this I will give you,' he said, 'if you will bow down and worship me.'" [Matthew 4:8—9] It was a way for Jesus to win without years of trekking through desert wastelands, without mocking opponents, and especially with no arrest, no beating, no scourging, no thorns, and no cross. What a deal! But Jesus didn't take it. Why? Because it's not just winning that matters. It's how you win. And so "Jesus said to him, 'Away from me, Satan! For it is written: "Worship the Lord your God, and serve him only."'" [Matthew 4:10] And serving a righteous God requires righteous means as well as righteous ends. That often is not a hallmark of politics.

Barack Obama once said about Senator Harry Reid, "I wouldn't have been president had it not been for your encouragement and support, and I wouldn't have got most of what I got done without your skill and determination." During the 2012 presidential campaign, Reid criticized Obama's Republican opponent, Mitt Romney, for not paying taxes for ten years, thereby tainting Romney in the eyes of many voters. It was a lie, and Reid knew it. When asked about his lie after his party had won the presidency that year, Reid simply said, "It worked, didn't it?"

"Winning" is the objective of politics. "Truth" is not. This is another inevitable flaw of the party system. The party leaders and their politicians need to win, so they train their members to pursue victory instead of truth. But this sullies us all. Think about what happens to us when the antithesis of truth becomes acceptable in order to win. Who is the "Father of Lies?" Who is "the Way, the Truth, and the Life?" If lies become an acceptable tactic, then we become agents of Satan and enemies of Christ.

And that is politics. And it is not just Democratic Party politics. After all, it was the Republicans who made the word, "Watergate" famous. Republican operatives broke into the campaign office of Nixon's opponent in the 1972 presidential election to obtain information about the Democratic Party's candidate and his campaign plans—even though polling indicated the Democrat had virtually no chance of winning.

Political operations in our own age have become even worse— much worse. Lies and hypocrisy have become the preferred method of operation for the political parties, while they sew division and hate among Americans. The parties conjure an "us versus them" scenario and then try to scrape together enough of "us" to add up to 51% while turning the other 49% into enemies— and deplorable ones at that. That tactic may work to help a party win, but it causes the nation to lose. There is no "us" and "them" in God's eyes. It's all "us", and we're all family.

As Christians, we know we will win. We know how the story ends. We do not need to compromise merely to put a few more points on the scoreboard. Let our standard be righteousness, and let us pursue righteous ends outside of traditional politics. How do we do this without relying on conventional politics and political parties?

Discussion

"In such a [political] system, righteousness is often not an objective at all. At best, it is a slogan." Give some examples that illustrate this.

The author argues that *"serving a righteous God requires righteous means as well as righteous ends."* Is it acceptable to support a politician who can accomplish good ends even though his personal behavior is morally despicable? Do you think God would agree with your answer?

"'Winning' is the objective of politics. 'Truth' is not...If lies become an acceptable tactic, then we become agents of Satan and enemies of Christ." Is a defeat at the polls acceptable as long as you stay true to God and the truth? Is a victory at the polls acceptable if you had to resort to lies and ungodliness to accomplish it?

If *"There is no 'us' and 'them' in God's eyes. It's all 'us', and we're all family"*, then how does this limit our political tactics when dealing with the opposition?

"As Christians, we know we will win. We know how the story ends. We do not need to compromise merely to put a few more points on the scoreboard." What do you think this means as a practical matter when dealing with political action?

CHAPTER SIXTEEN:

The Ark

"The Lord saw how great the wickedness of the human race had become on the earth, and that every inclination of the thoughts of the human heart was only evil all the time. The Lord regretted that he had made human beings on the earth, and his heart was deeply troubled. So the Lord said, 'I will wipe from the face of the earth the human race I have created—and with them the animals, the birds and the creatures that move along the ground—for I regret that I have made them.' But Noah found favor in the eyes of the Lord." [Genesis 6:5—8]

Sounds a lot like today, but it wasn't. It was a long time ago. Still, there are some important lessons this account of "The Flood" teaches to us today, and we would be well-advised to pay attention. First, God is watching. Nothing escapes His notice, and nothing escapes His judgment. He will respond to wickedness. He has to. A righteous God cannot just look the other way without losing His credentials for righteousness. He expects a lot from His creation, and it breaks His heart when we don't live up to expectations. He also loves His creation, and although He must deal with wickedness, He is a God of hope and redemption who looks for ways to make the future better than the past. This, however, cannot happen unless the creation ultimately returns to fellowship with Him and obedience to Him. Back then, God found one righteous man and built His plan for the future around him. There is no reason to believe that He won't do it again, but first, He must find a righteous man—or nation.

We used to be that nation. The benefits were stunning. God helped a ragtag collection of farmers and merchants defeat the most powerful empire on Earth at the time, and then go on to establish a new foundation of government which supported and guided us to become history's strongest, wealthiest, and greatest nation. As George Washington said in his first inaugural address, "Every step by which they [we] have advanced to the character of an independent nation seems to have been distinguished by some token of providential agency...." In other words, God got us here; and why wouldn't He? We had appealed "to the Supreme Judge of the world for the rectitude of our intentions" and put our "firm reliance on the Protection of Divine Providence...." We turned to God. We pledged to do it His way. It worked. And it continued to work for nearly one-and-three-quarters centuries. But then came the doctrine of Separation of Church and State which quickly morphed into the idea that we had to remove God from government. And that is exactly what we did. And just as the benefits of serving God were stunning, the curses of abandoning Him have been even more stunning. There is scarcely a single indicator of national nobility which has not declined dramatically since the inception of Separation of Church and State. Family decay, divorce, crime, all manner of perversion, corruption, political dysfunction, deep divisions among the elements of our populace, collapse of our educational system, the loss of preeminence in science, technology, economic might, etc., etc., etc. As Garlow and Barton summed up in *This Precarious Moment* [Salem Books 2018, p. 215] "The de-Christianizing of American public life and the open rejection of our historic Biblical foundations has resulted in a nation exploding in crime, sexual anarchy, wrecked homes and lives, now leaving massive human pain and carnage in its wake." Even military mastery has been lost. Think about it. Up to 1947 (when the Court case instituting Separation of Church and State occurred), the United States had never lost a war. Since then the only war we clearly won was the Grenada conflict back in October, 1983, where we showed a thing or two to a tiny Caribbean nation with an active army of about 1,500 soldiers and no modern air defenses. The history of the United States obviously supports the contention that with God you cannot lose; without God you cannot win.

We are crippled by a bi-polar approach to social, political, and economic reform. We tend to think only in terms of political action, and then only in terms of action through the Republican Party Corporation or the Democratic Party Corporation. If either of these parties had an answer, we wouldn't be in the mess we have today. Politics and politicians have failed us. We need to look elsewhere for solutions. Combining the wisdom of two prominent Americans already quoted in this book should illuminate our path to rebuilding America the good, the great, and the Godly.

In his first inaugural address, Washington prophesied "the propitious smiles of Heaven, can never be expected on a nation that disregards the eternal rules of order and right, which Heaven itself has ordained...." Mark Twain, although not a renowned Christian, also prophesied, "It will be conceded...that a Christian's first duty is to God. It then follows, as a matter of course, that it is his duty to carry his Christian code of morals to the polls and vote them. If Christians should vote their duty to God at the polls, they would carry every election and do it with ease.... If the Christians of America could be persuaded to vote God and a clean ticket, it would bring about a moral revolution that would be incalculably beneficent. It would save the country."

Combining the wisdom of Washington and Twain provides a template for saving America now: return to God, serve Him faithfully, make Him and His word the heart of our message to America, vote accordingly, win.

In a nutshell, we need to reach out to Bible-based individuals and organizations of faith, educate them, organize them, mobilize them. "It would save the country." Forget the elephant and the donkey. Embrace the Lion and the Lamb.

Thousands of years ago, a righteous man was noticed by God who directed him. That righteous man listened to God, and built a bridge to the future by building an ark for his loved ones. Thousand of years later, a righteous people are being noticed by God who wants them to listen to Him and become His instruments for building another bridge to the future. This time that instrument will not be a boat. It must be a nation: the United States of America, which can become God's instrument, once again, for lighting the way, revealing the truth, and ennobling life on Earth.

Discussion

"Back then [the time of Noah], God found one righteous man and built His plan for the future around him. There is no reason to believe that He won't do it again, but first, He must find a righteous man—or nation." A righteous God always builds with righteousness. Can we expect to be a tool of God if we remain unrighteous?

"If either of these parties [Republicans and Democrats] had an answer, we wouldn't be in the mess we have today. Politics and politicians have failed us. We need to look elsewhere for solutions." Do you agree? Is there another way to explain many of the problems of America today other than by blaming our two dominant parties? If not them, who?

The author argues that *"Combining the wisdom of Washington and Twain provides a template for saving America now: return to God, serve Him faithfully, make Him and His word the heart of our message to America, vote accordingly, win."* Do you think this would work? If not, why not? If so, are you willing to join the fight?

The author believes *"the United States of America…can become God's instrument, once again, for lighting the way, revealing the truth, and ennobling life on Earth."* Do you see another alternative?

CHAPTER SEVENTEEN:

On Earth as it is in Heaven

The perfect prayer was given to us by the Perfect Man, Jesus. It is recorded in the sixth chapter of Matthew and in a less familiar form in the eleventh chapter of Luke. Among other things, we are to pray "your kingdom come, your will be done, on earth as it is in heaven." [Matthew 6:10] Jesus didn't come only to provide an escape hatch on the chute to Hell. He also gave us directions for creating the "Kingdom of Heaven" here on Earth. As a nation, we used to do a much better job of following those directions than we do now; and as pointed out in the preceding chapter, we also used to enjoy a great deal more of God's blessings then than we do now. My proposition is simple: go back to doing it God's way. This is how we can reclaim and restore what was once ours; namely, America the Good, the Great, and the Godly.

Our mission should be to rebuild the United States of America spiritually, politically, and economically according to Biblical principles and the ideals of the Founders. By the way, the "ideals of the Founders" were largely inspired by "Biblical principles", so our primary focus needs to be on the Bible. Let's continue the analogy of the Ark to see how we can do this. First, God gave Noah very specific directions for building the Ark. That is because the Ark had a very specific mission. Just any craft would not work, and that should surprise no one. You don't design and build a speedboat to carry thousands of tons of cargo across the ocean. Similarly, you don't expect a massive supertanker to win a race against speedboats. Speedboats and supertankers are intended for very different tasks. Accordingly, they are very different in their design and structure. So, what kind of craft do we need to construct in order to rebuild America?

As I have already written, we need to break free from the notion that we should address all our problems via politics, politicians, and political parties. This is a trap, and like most other traps, it doesn't end well for those caught within the trap. Politicians and political parties are not good at taking care of people. They are good at taking care of themselves. Christians and Jews are good at taking care of people, even at the expense of taking care of themselves. Both the Old and New Testaments proclaim our responsibility to care for one another—especially the most disadvantaged among us. Politicians and political parties may say they are interested in doing this, but their real motive is the accumulation of power for the purposes of the power elite—which both major parties serve. Christians and Jews, on the other hand, pursue the objective of helping others to honor God and to ennoble their own lives through righteousness.

We need to build working associations among individuals and organizations of faith to tackle our social problems. Homelessness, poverty, healthcare, the causes of crime, elder care, child care, re-cycling, addictions, and improvement in education, for example, are all better served by Godly people and organizations than political ones. Politicians will pursue these goals to collect more power. Christians and Jews will pursue these goals to solve the problem. Imagine the leaders and members of churches, synagogues, and Godly charities getting together regularly to solve their communities' challenges. Imagine how motivated they will be to address problems that are on their own doorsteps. And imagine how much more money would be available for these activities if we stopped sending so much of the wealth we create to various government agencies to be dispersed on manifold government boondoggles. Instead of city councils and county boards of supervisors, we should turn to interfaith commissions to devise, engineer, implement, and administer programs to heal our communities and their citizens. [See Appendix A] Successful policies and operations in one locality will be shared with other ones by word-of-mouth and through denominational channels. Local districts will start to compete with each other to build better neighborhoods. This is greatly preferable to political parties competing with each other to expand their own power at the expense of the other party. Unity (e pluribus unum) will again become our maxim instead of division (e unum pluribus).

As this movement for the interfaith management of our communities grows, the need for—and size of—government can shrink, with all the attendant blessings. As I wrote back in Chapter Thirteen, "Governments operate by making, administering, and adjudicating laws. Laws, by there very nature, almost always work to limit freedoms." The smaller the government, the greater our liberty. I also wrote in Chapter Thirteen that almost no one can think of anything that the government does effectively and efficiently. Among other things this means that we spend a great deal of money (our money) to obtain solutions that don't happen. With local control of our programs run by people who are readily available to us (like pastors, priests, rabbis, and lay volunteers) I think we can expect a great deal more efficacy and efficiency, and with a lower price tag.

How do we get to the point where we can do this? Simple: do this! We don't need to wait for some legislation or Constitutional amendment to begin this process. Just do it. Churches, synagogues, and Godly charitable organizations in a locale can get together to start the process. Good places to begin are in areas such as homelessness, healthcare, pregnancy centers, and schools. [See Appendices A, B, and C] Don't think that this must be accomplished at the exclusion of local government agencies. Initially, we should work in fellowship with them because they are the ones currently dealing with most of these issues. But as the process evolves, the interfaith commissions will play a bigger and bigger role while the role of the government agencies will decrease.

In addition to assuming responsibility for handling many problems and challenges currently managed by government agencies, we need to take a greater role in running and influencing these government agencies themselves. Even as this plan progresses, we will never end the need for government. Our goal must be to shrink government by assuming many of its responsibilities and to influence the operation of the government agencies which remain. We need to infuse them with Biblical values and people, and we do this by urging Bible-believers to run for office and then by having Bible-believing people vote for them.

As we use the example of the Ark to guide our reclamation and restoration of America, we began with the design of the Ark. We must build a craft that is capable of accomplishing our Godly mission. That requires a shift away from politics and political parties and toward Biblical institutions and individuals. We still will need an organization—much like a political party, but without the emphasis on the "part." Our organization will seek to bless the whole nation by faithfully serving God. This should be an alliance or coalition of Godly individuals and organizations that work to elect righteous people with righteous ideas for reconstituting our communities, states, and nation. Furthermore, we must vet, recruit, and support our candidates for public office.

Next, we must mobilize the Christian community to register to vote and go to the polls. As Mark Twain said, "If Christians should vote their duty to God at the polls, they would carry every election and do it with ease....It would save the country." But that is a very big "if." A huge percentage of Christians are not even registered to vote. This means they are completely unable to influence an election. Of those registered, another huge percentage do not vote. A survey conducted by George Barna in September of 2024—less than two months before a major election—found that 79% of Americans self-identify as a person of faith or are associated with a recognized religious faith, such as Christianity, Judaism, Mormonism, Islam, etc. This amounts to about 212 million American adults. Of this group, only 51% said they are likely to vote while 49% said they are not likely to vote. This means that roughly 104 million people of faith did not intend to vote in 2024. The Associated Press reported that in the 2024 election, Donald Trump received 77,297,721 popular votes while Kamala Harris received 75,009,338. The number of eligible people of faith who did not intend to vote overwhelms the winning number chalked up by the victor of the 2024 presidential election. If just 75% of those who did not plan on voting changed their minds, they, alone, would constitute a larger assembly than Trump's total number of votes. Twain was right and still is. "If Christians should vote their duty to God at the polls, they would carry every election and do it with ease...."

So, why don't we vote? Barna's survey also explored that question. Of the 41 million born-again Christians who didn't expect to vote, 68% said they were not interested in politics, 57% disliked all the major candidates, 55% felt none of the candidates reflected their views, 52% thought one vote didn't make a difference, 50% thought the election was too controversial, 48% believed the election would be rigged or felt they didn't know enough about the candidates to make an informed decision, 36% thought their preferred candidate couldn't win. We are doing a poor job of educating our fellow Christians about their responsibility to bring Christ into the world. And by "we", I'm afraid the lion's share of that responsibility rests with our church leaders. Allow me to add another category to the ones cited by Charles Finney quoted in Chapter Ten: "If there is ignorance and indifference among the people about their responsibility to elect Godly people to public office, the pulpit is responsible for it."

So, the "ark" represents the organization we must construct to carry us through the storm to sail from where we are as a nation to where we must go. Next, let's consider the three classes of passengers on the Ark: the captain, the crew, and the cargo. Each has a specific and indispensable role to play for the Ark to accomplish its mission.

The Captain

Every ship needs a captain. His job is to deliver his craft to its destination while tending to the well-being of his cargo and crew. This requires the captain to be a person of vision. He must know where he is going even when he cannot see where he is going. This often requires navigational aids. For a captain at sea, this likely will consist of heavenly markers (like the North Star or the Southern Cross), a sextant, and a compass. For the captain of a people, this will necessarily include the Bible. Even when a captain cannot see his destination, God can. Trust Him. Follow Him. The leader of our nation must be a person familiar with the Bible and committed to following it.

A captain also must be familiar with handling rough seas. Problems are inevitable—especially when there are those who want to keep you from arriving at your destination. Our national leaders must have the experience and resolve to know how to weather stormy seas and deliver their cargo and crew safely to the other side. Here again, familiarity with the Bible will be indispensable. It teaches the values that enable a leader to persevere through troubles. The most important of these values is to listen to God and to obey Him. Notice, Noah never attended a seafarers' academy—as far as we know, he never even paddled a raft across a pond—but he navigated his massive ship through stormy seas for months and delivered his cargo safely to its destination by obeying the word of the Lord. Moses never went to a military academy—as far as we know, he couldn't march a squad across a drill field—but he prevailed against mighty pharaoh and his army by obeying the word of the Lord. The Bible offers many other examples of the blessings that result from obeying God. It's good to know that your coach has a successful track record—and our Coach is undefeated.

Good leaders also must be inspirational. The path often will be difficult. The challenges will often seem insurmountable and dangerous. The crew may lose courage and resolve under these circumstances. At such times, faith in the leader will be indispensable. The crew must trust that the leader knows what he is doing and is worthy of admiration and obedience. Nothing will inspire a Godly crew more than the knowledge that their captain is a Godly and righteous person. Accordingly, a leader must tend to the spiritual enrichment of his crew and, even more importantly, must be known to be a righteous person himself. The righteousness of the leader is not only necessary to win the confidence and admiration of the crew, it is necessary to secure the blessings of God. Oh, how we have failed in this regard, and we all have paid the price. As we are pointedly reminded in Proverbs 29:2, "When the righteous thrive, the people rejoice; when the wicked rule, the people groan."

What are some of the qualities and qualifications we should demand in a leader? The Bible gives us ample guidance in this regard. Let's consider a few passages.

In Exodus 18:21 we are told to "select capable men from all the people—men who fear God, trustworthy men who hate dishonest gain—and appoint them as officials over thousands, hundreds, fifties and tens." This passage gives a broad definition of "capable men"—or men "beyond reproach", as we find in an other translation. We find this same advice continued in the New Testament. Titus 1:7-9 says,

> "Since an overseer manages God's household, he must be blameless—not overbearing, not quick-tempered, not given to drunkenness, not violent, not pursuing dishonest gain. Rather, he must be hospitable, one who loves what is good, who is self-controlled, upright, holy and disciplined. He must hold firmly to the trustworthy message as it has been taught, so that he can encourage others by sound doctrine and refute those who oppose it."

This theme is repeated in 1 Timothy 3:1-7.

> "Whoever aspires to be an overseer desires a noble task. Now the overseer is to be above reproach, faithful to his wife, temperate, self-controlled, respectable, hospitable, able to teach, not given to drunkenness, not violent but gentle, not quarrelsome, not a lover of money. He must manage his own family well and see that his children obey him, and he must do so in a manner worthy of full respect. (If anyone does not know

how to manage his own family, how can he take care of God's church?) He must not be a recent convert, or he may become conceited and fall under the same judgment as the devil. He must also have a good reputation with outsiders, so that he will not fall into disgrace and into the devil's trap."

Let us linger a moment to further consider the requirement that "He must not be a recent convert...." We want our leaders to have a lengthy track record for living a Godly life. This works to confirm that righteousness is a way of life and not a convenient affectation. A recent convert may have sniffed the winds and perceived that an association with and reputation for righteousness could work to his advantage. In cases like this, a Godly appearance is a con and not genuine. Furthermore, a recent convert may not have developed the habit of righteousness and may quickly revert to his previous tendencies when challenged.

Another trait of great leaders is that they must be humble servants of the led. Philippians 2:4 offers a test that most of our politicians would likely fail: "Do nothing out of selfish ambition or vain conceit. Rather, in humility value others above yourselves, not looking to your own interests but each of you to the interests of the others." This message recorded by the Apostle Paul was first preached by his Master, Jesus:

> "Jesus called them together and said, 'You know that those who are regarded as rulers of the Gentiles lord it over them, and their high officials exercise authority over them. Not so with you. Instead, whoever wants to become great among you must be your servant, and whoever wants to be first must be slave of all. For even the Son of Man did not come to be served, but to serve, and to give his life as a ransom for many.'" [Mark 10:42—45]

And let's be sure to recall some of Jesus' final instructions to Peter, recorded in John 21:17, "Feed my sheep." Feed the sheep, not fleece them. The leader exists to serve the interests of the led—not the other way around.

Both Republicans and Democrats can point to the other side of the aisle with valid charges of moral turpitude; for example, serial adultery, sexual assault, lies, perjury, fraud, hypocrisy, crooked business practices, obstruction of justice, and more. And both the Republicans and the Democrats would be correct. What has happened to us!?! The removal of God and the politicalization of our national lives have led us to tolerate all manner of depravity and wickedness—as long as our side wins. No! No one wins when evil prevails.

I have heard Christian commentators advise Christians to "vote defensively" or "strategically", which means to vote in such a manner as to limit the evil that can result from an election. Even Pope Francis has adopted this position. In remarks where he criticized both of the party candidates for the American presidential election of 2024, he said, "One should vote, and choose the lesser evil. Who is the lesser evil, the woman or man? I don't know." [Associated Press, September 14, 2024] In other words, if both parties offer candidates who are moral snakes, vote for the one with the weaker venom. Many people of faith have listened and followed this advice. And where has it gotten us? The lesser of two evils is still evil. We cannot prevent our slide into the pit as long as we remain satisfied with merely slowing our rate of descent. And rest assured, as long as we keep accepting the moral dung the political parties are serving up to us, the more they will continue to do exactly that; and where do you think that will lead? How do you think God feels about embracing the lesser of two evils? Did He ever once advise such a course? Then what makes you think the unchanging one suddenly changed His mind? Remember, you don't have to vote for one of the names on the ballot; but if you do, you can rest assured about the types of candidates you will see on the next ballot. If we keep validating the choices presented to us by the political parties, you can bet that you will see more of the same next time around. I have made a regular practice of placing write-in votes on my ballot for several years, even though I knew my candidate had no chance of winning the election. I have often been confronted by worldly wisemen who scolded me for "throwing away my vote." My response: "Don't you throw away your vote when you cast it for someone who can win an election, but lose the favor of God?" And, it seems, this is not just my belief. Jesus, Himself, said, "What good will it be for someone to gain the whole world, yet forfeit their soul?" [Matthew 16:26] I would much rather lose an election than God's favor; and if enough of us acted the same way, before long we will have candidates who can win an election and win the day for righteousness. If we have to thumb our nose at God in order to win a political election, the victory isn't worth it. We have a choice: God's way or the world's way. You can be certain of this—those choices will not end up at the same place. Righteousness—not the ability to win nor the favorable nature of one's platform—must be our first criterion for supporting a candidate. I think that is how God would want us to start.

"But Hebron", you may be thinking, "no candidate is perfect. Besides, God has often chosen imperfect men and women to be leaders of His people. Remember King David (an adulterer and murderer), King Solomon (encouraged idolatry and married outside of the tribes of Israel against God's instructions), King Saul, and even Samson (both prideful and disobedient). They all did some terrible things, yet God still chose them. You're being too demanding by insisting on righteousness as our first criterion for choosing a leader!"

Nice try, but that argument won't fly. First of all, of course no candidate is perfect. Of course God has chosen imperfect men and women to be leaders of His people. He has no alternative. "There is no one righteous, not even one….for all have sinned and fall short of the glory of God…." [Romans 3:10 & 23] If God had wanted perfectly obedient children, He would have—and could have—made human nature differently. (Ever think of why He didn't do that? But then, that is the subject for another book in itself.)

Second, I would have to disagree with you about God's alleged choices of moral reprobates to lead His children. God did NOT choose the aforementioned leaders <u>despite</u> their sins. David's sins of adultery and murder came <u>after</u> he was chosen by God. Solomon's sins of allowing and encouraging idolatry came <u>after</u> he was chosen by God. Saul's and Samson's sins came <u>after</u> they were chosen by God. God didn't choose an adulterer and murderer to be king of His people. He chose a pure-hearted shepherd boy composing hymns while tending his father's sheep. God didn't choose a lusty idolator to be king of His people. He chose a young man about twenty years old who above all else sought wisdom. God didn't choose a prideful, disobedient person to be the first king of His people. He chose a humble young man about thirty years old who hid from the call to royalty. God didn't choose a foolish, vengeful hulk to free His people from foreign oppressors. He chose an unborn child to whom He gave great powers. And in each of these cases, God punished them when they went astray. The prophet Nathan told David, "because by doing this you have shown utter contempt for the Lord, the son born to you will die." [2 Samuel 12:14] Solomon would suffer for his disobedience. "The

Lord became angry with Solomon because his heart had turned away from the Lord, the God of Israel, who had appeared to him twice. Although he had forbidden Solomon to follow other gods, Solomon did not keep the Lord's command. So the Lord said to Solomon, 'Since this is your attitude and you have not kept my covenant and my decrees, which I commanded you, I will most certainly tear the kingdom away from you and give it to one of your subordinates.'" [1 Kings 11:9-11] King Saul would lose both his kingdom and life for his insubordination. In 1 Kings 15:26 Samuel delivers the bad news to Saul. "You have rejected the word of the Lord, and the Lord has rejected you as king over Israel!" And in the case of Samson, "the Philistines seized him, gouged out his eyes and took him down to Gaza. Binding him with bronze shackles, they set him to grinding grain in the prison." [Judges 16:21]

God did not pick men who had committed great sins to be the leaders of His people. He chose men who later committed great sins, disobeying and disappointing God, and the consequences were disastrous for the unrighteous leaders and those they led.

Well, if "There is no one righteous, not even one", then what standard should we use to select our leaders? I'd recommend the same one used by college admission boards. A high school student does not need to have had perfect grades on every test and graded event since kindergarten in order to be admitted to the college of his choice. "A" and even "B" grades may be sufficient—and just for the last few years. But there is no way you're getting in with "Ds" and Fs." So, look for candidates who can at least score a "B" on the righteousness scale and forget those with "Ds" and "Fs." I realize that is a bit vague, but I think the principle is sound. The people will have to decide what constitutes a "B", and to do this accurately, they must study the Bible.

The vote of a Christian is not merely a declaration of which candidate we think will do the better job. It is an endorsement of a candidate's spiritual character. Even when we choose righteous leaders, things may go badly. If we choose unrighteous leaders, we can count on it.

The Crew

Shortly after my assignment as commanding officer of Company A, Fourth Tank Battalion, Fourth Marine Division, one of my senior non-commissioned officers (high-ranking enlisted men, for you non-military types) asked if he could talk with me. He felt there were areas where our unit could improve and suggested that I meet with all the other non-commissioned officers in the company because they had some ideas for reform. I immediately agreed, and we quickly scheduled a meeting. We talked for quite a while. My Marines had a number of excellent ideas. I immediately adopted many of them while others were instituted with some modifications to accommodate other factors; for example, because we had to work with other companies in the battalion. At the end of the meeting, everyone seemed pleased—not only that valuable ideas had been adopted and implemented, but because those offering these ideas had been listened to. After the meeting broke up, the same non-commissioned officer who had asked for the meeting stayed behind to thank me. He said they had asked the same thing of other incoming company commanders, but that I had been the only one who had agreed to meet. I was amazed. Even though I was the company commander—the boss, indeed, the small-"g" god should we go to combat—I knew that many of these Marines had more practical knowledge about running a tank company than I did. Why wouldn't I want to take advantage of all that experience? It paid off. Time after time, in both tactical and administrative matters, my company excelled and was recognized. I never failed to credit my team because, quite simply, they deserved it. I didn't excel. We did. Sometimes the greatest act of leadership is to get out of the way of your talented crew members—or, at least, to empower them.

This is another vital job of a good captain; namely, take advantage of the expertise available to you. "We" is greater than "I." But before a captain can take advantage of the crew's expertise, the crew must first develop their skills. A captain cannot sail a ship alone. He must acquire and train a talented crew. The crew must rise to the challenge of developing the necessary skills to maneuver and maintain the craft. They must be committed to their mission. They must be willing to work hard—and even sacrifice—to accomplish their mission.

We Christians must see ourselves as crew members of our Captain's vessel. We must be loyal to Him. We must be well-trained. We must be committed, capable, and hard-working. What does this mean? Study. Read the Bible and other spiritual treatises. Belong to a congregation. Attend Bible classes. Pray. Live righteously. Serve in ministries where you feel a special gift. Offer advice and support to your local leaders, and be ready to step in if called to lead.

We had a saying in the Marines, which, I suspect, was shared by other organizations—especially those where accomplishing the mission was given foremost importance: Lead, follow, or get the heck out of the way. (Actually, we didn't say "heck" but this is a Christian living book, so I occasionally must sacrifice accuracy for propriety.) Ultimately, it is a team effort that achieves results. When done rightly, it often will be hard to see where leadership ends and followership begins.

The Cargo

And then, there is the reason why the ship was built in the first place: the cargo. For Noah, it was his family and the critters. For us, it is our family and the rest of God's family. We are charged with bringing all of God's children safely to our home port. "Therefore go and make disciples of all nations...." [Matthew 28:19] This is why the ship was built. This is why the crew exists. This is the captain's mission. This is why we endure the risks: to bring our brothers and sisters safely home. This requires not only the skill of the captain and the hard, capable work of the crew. It requires the ship that can accomplish this mission, and our ark is named the United States of America. We must be the vessel that knows the way, shows the way, goes the way; indeed, is the way. No nation on Earth has ever accomplished the good that we have, but our job is not over yet. Our Father and His children depend upon us. We must be the vessel that dares to set out across dark and dangerous waters. We must be not only a lifeboat but also a battleship. We must seek the lost, the marooned, the swamped, the drowning. We must fight the marauders of malevolence. We are made of God-stuff, and we will answer His call. We will be true to His commission. We will fulfill our God-given destiny, because we are Americans, and that is what Americans do.

Discussion

Do you think that "doing it God's way" can restore "America the Good, the Great, and the Godly"? If not, what can?

The author states that *"Our mission should be to rebuild the United States of America spiritually, politically, and economically according to Biblical principles and the ideals of the Founders."* Do you agree? Can you think of a better mission statement for Americans?

The author claims that *"Politicians and political parties are not good at taking care of people. They are good at taking care of themselves."* Do you agree? Can you cite evidence for your belief? If the author is correct, then how smart is it for us to trust our well-being to politicians?

The author claims there is a "power elite" which both major parties serve. Do you think this is conspiratorial claptrap, or truth? Throughout the ages, many historians and other political observers have believed in the existence of a secretive power elite. If this is not true, why would they think it is?

"We need to build working associations among individuals and organizations of faith to tackle our social problems." Think about and discuss how this could be accomplished in your community.

"Instead of city councils and county boards of supervisors, we should turn to interfaith commissions to devise, engineer, implement, and administer programs to heal our communities and their citizens." Discuss why this could be a good idea. Discuss the problems that could result from such a system. How could you avoid or solve those problems?

"With local control of our programs run by people who are readily available to us (like pastors, priests, rabbis, and lay volunteers) I think we can expect a great deal more efficacy and efficiency, and with a lower price tag." Why would such a system work better than the current political one characterized by city councils and county boards of supervisors?

"Our goal must be to shrink government by assuming many of its responsibilities and to influence the operation of the government agencies which remain. We need to infuse them with Biblical

values and people, and we do this by urging Bible-believers to run for office and then by having Bible-believing people vote for them." In a later section, the author argues that we are not doing a very good job of this. How can we do a better job? Existing congregations need to be a part of this process. How can we get them to do a better job? Would you work with your congregation to accomplish this?

The author argues that, as we work to rebuild America the good, the great, and the Godly, "*We still will need an organization— much like a political party, but without the emphasis on the 'part.'*" How would this organization be similar to existing political parties? How would it be different?

Look at the reasons given by evangelical Christians for not voting. Do any of these apply to you? Do you think that God wants us to show up at the polls on election day in order to influence the outcome of the election and, thereby, the nature of our nation? If not, why wouldn't He?

The author believes "*We are doing a poor job of educating our fellow Christians about their responsibility to bring Christ into the world. And by 'we', I'm afraid the lion's share of that responsibility rests with our church leaders.*" Do you think you need to talk with your church leaders about this? If yes, will you?

"*The leader of our nation must be a person familiar with the Bible and committed to following it.*" Do you believe this? What would happen if our national leaders are not people "familiar with the Bible and committed to following it"?

The author writes that "our Coach [God] is undefeated", so why wouldn't we want to listen to Him?

"*The righteousness of the leader is not only necessary to win the confidence and admiration of the crew, it is necessary to secure the blessings of God.*" When was the last time you heard one of the main political parties advertise the righteousness of their candidates? Do you think they are missing something?

Review the qualifications for a good "overseer" listed in 1 Timothy 3:1-7. How have our recent leaders scored by this standard? What grade would you give them—"A" through "F"?

The author points out that some Christian commentators advise us to choose the "lesser evil" if neither of the candidates offered to us is righteous. "*How do you think God feels about embracing the lesser of two evils? Did He ever once advise such a course? Then what makes you think the unchanging one suddenly changed His mind?"*

The author says he would rather vote for a righteous candidate who has no chance of winning than to vote for someone who can win, but is unrighteous. When confronted by those who argue that he has thrown away his vote, the author replies, *"Don't you throw away your vote when you cast it for someone who can win an election, but lose the favor of God?"* How do you feel about this? Do you think your vote is not only an expression of who is the better candidate but also a personal endorsement of that person? Can you personally endorse some of the people you vote for? Could you face God and endorse them?

Do you agree with the author when he writes *"Righteousness—not the ability to win nor the favorable nature of one's platform—must be our first criterion for supporting a candidate. I think that is how God would want us to start"*?

Some argue that God has chosen some very flawed individuals to lead His people. The author argues that He did not. God chose them when they were still relatively righteous. They became "flawed" later, and often suffered greatly for it—and so did their nation. The author believes we must first demand righteous leaders, and then watch them closely to make sure they do not stray from the Godly path, because we are likely to fall with them when they sin. Do you agree or disagree?

We are part of God's team. What does that mean to you, and how can you be a better team member?

The United States, *"must be the vessel that knows the way, shows the way, goes the way; indeed, is the way...We must be the vessel that dares to set out across dark and dangerous waters. We must seek the lost, the marooned, the swamped, the drowning. We must fight the marauders of malevolence. We are made of God-stuff, and we will answer His call. We will be true to His commission. We will fulfill our God-given destiny, because we are Americans, and that is what Americans do."* Do you think this is an old-fashioned, outdated notion, or is it a call to action?

CHAPTER EIGHTEEN:

Can This Work?

America is great because she is good. If America ever ceases to be good, America will cease to be great. This is one of the main themes of this book. One of the main contentions of this book is that the United States Supreme Court case, Everson vs the Board of Education in 1947, was a watershed event that began a process which has exiled God from government, expelled Him from our schools, and minimized His influence in much of the rest of our society. In short, America has ceased to be good.

America faces a myriad of problems that seem increasingly intractable. Furthermore, the methodology we have embraced for solving those problems—namely, politics, political parties, and politicians—obviously is not working. We are arguably more divided now than at any other time except the Civil War. Everyone wants solutions; but if we keep doing what we've been doing, we're going to keep getting what we've been getting—and, quite simply, that is not acceptable.

The Founders and Framers created a government that was quite remarkable and unique; and as we have seen, they made God the center of everything they did and the foundation of everything they built. It worked. America became great because it was good. There is no reason it cannot happen again. I have urged us to turn away from traditional politics and turn toward a faith-based approach to solving our problems—specifically, a Bible-based approach. To put an even finer point to this, this should be a blatantly Christian approach. It is what the Founders and Framers did, and if we seek to replicate their success, we need to copy their methodology. To repeat the observation of Patrick Henry, "It cannot be emphasized too clearly and too often that this nation was founded, not by religionists, but by Christians; not on religion, but on the gospel of Jesus Christ."

However, even this spiritual approach offers no guarantee of success. Let's face it, Christians have a long history that has often been characterized by injustice and savage aggression against outsiders and each other. I'm sure the opponents of my proposal will be quick to point this out. Let me be equally quick to point out that this is not the inevitable consequence of Christianity. It is the inevitable consequence of being human. Human nature is contentious and savage; and that savagery bubbles up—no, it erupts—into virtually every human activity. It twists and distorts and ravages almost everything we attempt. Rather than ameliorating this, our philosophies, our ideologies, our religions generally become the tool of this savagery. But if there is any hope to overcome the brutality of humanity, it will bubble up—no, it will erupt—from a philosophy, an ideology, a religion that teaches love, sanctifies life, and connects us with a good and loving Father God—and nothing does this better than Christianity. It is our greatest hope. If we cannot save America through Christian means, then, I am afraid, we cannot save America. We will be destined to devolve into just another barbaric culture clothed, briefly, in resplendent raiments. God, help us.

And that is precisely the path we must tread. Aspire higher! We must humble ourselves and pray and seek His face and turn from our wicked ways. Then, God will help us, and this is our only hope.

Discussion

"I have urged us to turn away from traditional politics and turn toward a faith-based approach to solving our problems—specifically, a Bible-based approach. To put an even finer point to this, this should be a blatantly Christian approach. It is what the Founders and Framers did, and if we seek to replicate their success, we need to copy their methodology." Do you agree, or do you think things have changed so much that what worked before will not work now? If we do adopt a "blatantly Christian approach" to remaking America, will it constitute a violation of First Amendment protections for religious liberties? Did it before?

The author acknowledges that Christians *"have a long history that has often been characterized by injustice and savage aggression against outsiders and each other."* However, he argues that this is not an *"inevitable consequence of Christianity"*, but rather of human nature which erupts *"into virtually every human activity."* He follows up by arguing *"if there is any hope to overcome the brutality of humanity, it will bubble up—no, it will erupt—from a philosophy, an ideology, a religion that teaches love, sanctifies life, and connects us with a good and loving Father God—and nothing does this better than Christianity. It is our greatest hope…And that is precisely the path we must tread."* Do you agree, or is there another way? If so, what?

CHAPTER NINETEEN:

Trenton

On Christmas night, 1776, George Washington gathered the remaining bits and pieces of his nearly shattered army and boarded anything he could find that would float in order to cross the ice-choked Delaware River. He had been conducting a desperate fighting delay action since getting booted off of Long Island in New York the previous August. The weather was horrible and nearly scuttled his plans. Yet despite all the obstacles, he managed to get to the other side of the river. Washington formed his assault units and rode up and down the nearly mile long column of troops urging them to continue despite the freezing winter weather. Participants recalled the blood-stained snow painted by the shredded feet of his shoeless soldiers. Shortly after 8 o'clock on the morning of December 26, three columns formed to begin their attack upon the expert and vicious Hessians who were assisting the British. Washington led the middle column. Three Hessian regiments quickly formed to repulse the attackers. The Hessian commander, Colonel Johann Rall, ordered repeated counterattacks which Washington skillfully repulsed. Rall was mortally wounded, and many of his veteran troops fled in the face of the withering Patriot attack. In only one hour of fighting, the Continental army captured nearly 900 Hessian soldiers and officers along with a large supply of muskets, bayonets, swords, and cannons. Less than two weeks later, on January 3, 1777, Washington's soldiers attacked and defeated British forces near Princeton, New Jersey. The Patriot cause had reason to continue the fight.

On the morning of December 25, 1776, most of Washington's troops only expected to serve in the Continental Army a few more days. Their enlistments would soon expire, and the Patriot cause seemed hopeless. They were ready to quit and go home. Perhaps you felt the same way this morning. Don't quit. Our Trenton is just around the corner. God never loses. All we have to do is show up, stay faithful, obey our Commander, and prepare for the victory party. Remember, you are not alone. There are more of us than there are of them. Remember, "With man this is impossible, but with God all things are possible." [Matthew 19:26]

I remember a trip I made in December to the Post Office a few years ago. I was mailing a Christmas package and needed the assistance of a postal clerk to see how much it would cost and to purchase the necessary postage. The clerk was polite, but reserved. Upon finishing our transaction I smiled and wished her a "Merry Christmas." Her eyes popped, and her face almost exploded with joy. She returned with a bold "And merry Christmas to you, too." As a quasi-government agency, I knew managers had made sure to remove anything that hinted at the real reason for the season and that, undoubtedly, the employees had been instructed not to mention the Christ part of Christmas. But I had been the first to say the "C-word." I had opened the door, and the once-stolid clerk charged through it. I believe her behavior is likely characteristic of most Christians in America today. We have been beaten down and told to shut up. Christianity is something you do on Sunday morning, and only in a building with an plus sign on top of it. And as long as we do what we have been told, we will remain joyless and defeated. Well, just as I gave that postal clerk permission to proclaim Christ, Jesus has given us permission to do likewise. And we had better listen. All is at stake. What do we have to fear when we know we cannot lose?

The final stanza of the first verse of our national anthem asks a vital question. "O say, does that star-spangled banner yet wave o'er the land of the free and the home of the brave?" Does it? Will it? Every generation of American has had to answer that question. Now, it is our turn. And the best way to succeed at this is to remember the fourth verse of our national anthem:

"O thus be it ever when freemen shall stand

Between their lov'd home and the war's desolation!

Blest with vict'ry and peace may the heav'n rescued land

Praise the power that hath made and preserv'd us a nation!

Then conquer we must, when our cause it is just,

And this be our motto - "In God is our trust,"

And the star-spangled banner in triumph shall wave

O'er the land of the free and the home of the brave."

"In God is our trust", or, as our currency proclaims, "In God we trust." Christians have what America needs. Don't withhold it! To paraphrase Charles E. Weller, "Now is the time for all good Christians to come to the aid of their country." Yes, we have what America needs, and to withhold it would earn the eternal condemnation of our forefathers, our children, their children, the "huddled masses yearning to breathe free", and our God. America must once again become the Ark of the world—an escape from evil; a refuge for the righteous; and the harbinger of new life. We have nothing to fear. Without God, we cannot win. With God, we cannot lose. Embrace the victory! "Arise, shine, for your light has come, and the glory of the LORD rises upon you. See, darkness covers the earth and thick darkness is over the peoples, but the Lord rises upon you and his glory appears over you. Nations will come to your light, and kings to the brightness of your dawn." [Isaiah 60:1—3]

Arise, America, you are the hope of the world. You are the apple of God's eye. He longs to forgive our sin, heal our land, and rebuild America the Good, the Great, and the Godly. Ask, and it shall be given to you. Seek and you shall find. Knock, and the door shall be opened to you. You are made of God stuff. Act like it. Put your shoulder to the stone that seals the sepulcher of our Godly nation, and unleash the Second American Revolution—the American Resurrection.

For God and country!

A New Beginning for Old Glory.

AMEN!

Discussion

"We have been told that "Christianity is something you do on Sunday morning, and only in a building with an plus sign on top of it. And as long as we do what we have been told, we will remain joyless and defeated. Well, just as I gave that postal clerk permission to proclaim Christ, Jesus has given us permission to do likewise. And we had better listen. All is at stake. What do we have to fear when we know we cannot lose?" Do you feel you should be quiet about your faith? Do you feel you should keep religion out of politics? Or do you feel that it is time to get over it and boldly march forward as Christian soldiers to rebuild America the good, the great, and the Godly?

"Christians have what America needs. Don't withhold it! To paraphrase Charles E. Weller, 'Now is the time for all good Christians to come to the aid of their country.' Yes, we have what America needs, and to withhold it would earn the eternal condemnation of our forefathers, our children, their children, the 'huddled masses yearning to breathe free', and our God." Pause a moment to consider the consequences to our nation, our children, and the world if Christians fail to rise up and take the lead in the next chapter of America's history.

"Without God, we cannot win. With God, we cannot lose." Do you believe this? Then, what are you waiting for? *"You are made of God stuff. Act like it. Put your shoulder to the stone that seals the sepulcher of our Godly nation, and unleash the Second American Revolution—the American Resurrection."*

APPENDICES

APPENDIX A:

COOPERATE,

COORDINATE, CONQUER

Someone from the faith community needs to arise, design, and coordinate the social, political, and economic activities of our people. For decades we have surrendered that responsibility to the politicians. They have failed. Why shouldn't we do it? And by "we" I mean the individuals and organizations that have committed to serve the God of the Bible. We have what Americans need. Let's give it to them.

A Christian leader begins by reaching out to other Christian and Jewish leaders in his community. He shares a vision for rebuilding America the Good, the Great, and the Godly; and he proposes that we start with the local community. He proposes that the heads of churches and synagogues, along with the leaders of other Biblical organizations and charities, meet bi-monthly to discuss the most pressing problems of their locality and to devise solutions to these problems. These problems may include such things as homelessness, crime, addiction, abuse of certain groups, education, bigotry, inadequacy of healthcare, urban decay, etc. After identifying the most serious and pressing problems, they begin to discuss ways to solve these problems. Consider cooperation with local government, but do not subordinate yourselves to them. After all, it has been the failure of local government that requires your action.

After identifying these problems, choose a very small number to begin your activities. Don't fritter away your efforts and resources on a wide array of difficulties. Focus and concentrate on one or two or three problems that seem likely candidates for progress.

Next, solicit ideas for addressing these problems. Don't exclude "wild ideas." Even though they may not be feasible, including them in the discussion might reveal possibilities that otherwise would be overlooked. Focus on the use of gifted volunteers to advance your solutions. For example, certain healthcare professionals like doctors, nurses, and therapists could volunteer to staff a clinic providing services to the poor and homeless. Don't exclude professionals outside the realm of conventional, Western healthcare. Acupuncturists, herbalists, craniosacral therapists, and Reiki masters have achieved impressive results without costly equipment and medicines. Attorneys and paralegals could offer legal services to the poor. Educators can provide tutoring services for children who need help with their studies but whose parents cannot afford to hire aides. Seek volunteers from among the trades —like plumbers, electricians, carpenters, landscapers, and auto mechanics—who could provide important services to the elderly and poor who could not otherwise afford them.

Look to see if there are existing government agencies that already are working in these areas. Meet with them, discuss the possibilities of working together, then follow through until you have a plan for accomplishing your goals. In the meantime, discuss your vision with members of your congregations and organizations. Solicit volunteers who have the talent and heart for the kind of service you intend to offer. Look for others who are in a position to help fund your activities.

Once you are nearing the point of implementing a plan, consult with various legal, tax, and insurance experts to discover and implement the various regulatory requirements associated with the care you intend to offer. Unfortunately, a big heart will not protect you from big trouble if your humanitarian efforts violate tax codes, civil mandates, or if you are liable for unintended injuries caused by volunteers. Hopefully, you can find professionals in these areas who will provide you with free or inexpensive advice and options.

Once you have achieved success in the few initial areas you chose, plan to perpetuate your service and success. Then, if you are able, move on to a new area or two. Just make sure you don't jeopardize existing programs by creating additional ones.

Very early in this process, you will need to create a governing board to oversee the operation of this organization. The first person to reach out to other leaders and organizations is a likely choice to be the initial leader of the group. Still, not all visionaries are good managers, so you will quickly want to identify and install leaders who can make things happen. You also need to consider whether you need to create some formal business or other type of organization to ensure your legality and avoid tax and other regulatory problems.

Finally, don't take "no" for an answer. Of course it will be difficult. Of course there will be problems. You must persist and prevail. God never quit because it was difficult, and neither should His servants.

APPENDIX B:

SCHOOL BOARD RESOLUTION

In the heyday of America, our public schools were powerful agents to instill those skills, lessons, and values that were necessary to create and preserve America the Good, the Great, and the Godly. Today, these schools often tug strongly in the opposite direction. The following school board resolution would re-institute the following:

(1) voluntary, non-denominational prayer at all school functions and at all school facilities, (2) install images of the Ten Commandments and the text of the Ten Commandments at all school functions and at all school facilities, and (3) teach the moral lessons expressed in the Ten Commandments in each elementary school class and in every language and civics class in grades six through twelve.

These practices are nothing new. In fact, they were quite common in our public schools before the false doctrine of "Separation of Church and State" was instituted in 1947. Re-instituting these policies and practices would go a long way to restore civility and civics in our schools. You are permitted by the author to use this resolution at your local and state school boards.

Whereas

John Adams said, "religion and virtue are the only foundations … of republicanism and of all free governments" and "Our Constitution was made only for a moral and religious people. It is wholly inadequate to the government of any other."

Patrick Henry said, "The great pillars of all government and social life … [are] virtue, morality, and religion" and "It cannot be emphasized too clearly and too often that this nation was founded, not by religionists, but by Christians; not on religion, but on the gospel of Jesus Christ."

Charles Carroll, signer of the Declaration of Independence said, "without morals a republic cannot subsist any length of time; they therefore who are decrying the Christian religion, whose morality is so sublime and pure … are undermining the solid foundation of morals, the best security for the duration of free governments."

John Hancock said, "all confidence must be withheld from the means we use and reposed only on that God who rules in the armies of heaven and without whose blessings the best human councils are but foolishness and all created power vanity."

George Washington, President of the Constitutional Convention, said, "Religion and morality are the essential pillars of civil society" and "true religion affords to government its surest support" and "it would be peculiarly improper to omit, in this first official act, [Washington's first inauguration as President of the United States] my fervent supplications to that Almighty Being who rules over the universe, who presides in the councils of nations, and whose providential aids can supply every human defect .... No people can be bound to acknowledge and adore the Invisible Hand which conducts the affairs of men more than those of the United States. Every step by which they have advanced to the character of an independent nation seems to have been distinguished by some token of providential agency.... we ought to be no less persuaded that the propitious smiles of Heaven can never be expected on a nation that disregards the eternal rules of order and right which Heaven itself has ordained" and "I am sure there never was a people who had more reason to acknowledge a Divine interposition in their affairs than those of the United States; and I should be pained to believe that they have forgotten that Agency which was so often manifested during our revolution, or that they failed to consider the omnipotence of that God who is alone able to protect them" and "Of all the dispositions and habits which lead to political prosperity, religion and morality are indispensable supports. In vain would that man claim the tribute of patriotism, who should labor to subvert these great pillars of human happiness.... And let us with caution indulge the supposition that morality can be maintained without religion. Whatever may be conceded to the influence of refined education on minds ... reason and experience both forbid us to expect that national morality can prevail, in exclusion of religious principle."

Noah Webster said, "the moral principle and precepts contained in the Scriptures ought to form the basis of all our civil constitutions and laws" and "the Christian religion, in its purity, is the basis, or rather the source of all genuine freedom in government ... and I am persuaded that no civil government of a republican form can exist and be durable in which the principles of that religion have not a controlling influence" and "The education of youth should be watched with the most scrupulous attention. It is much easier to introduce and establish an effectual system ... than to correct by penal statutes the ill effects of a bad system.... The education of youth ... lays the foundations on which both law and gospel rest for success."

Samuel Adams said, "Education ... leads the youth beyond mere outside show [and] will impress their minds with a profound reverence of the Deity.... It will excite in them a just regard to Divine revelation."

Alexander Hamilton, signer of the Constitution, said, "the law ... dictated by God Himself is, of course, superior in obligation to any other. It is binding over all the globe, in all countries, and at all times. No human laws are of any validity if contrary to this."

Rufus King, signer of the Constitution, said, the "law established by the Creator ... extends over the whole globe, is everywhere and at all times binding upon mankind .... [This] is the law of God by which he makes his way known to man and is paramount to all human control."

Abraham Baldwin, signer of the Constitution, said, "free government ... can only be happy when the public principle and opinions are properly directed ... by religion and education. It should therefore be among the first objects of those who wish well to the national prosperity to encourage and support the principles of religion and morality."

Gouverneur Morris, signer of the Constitution said, "Religion is the only solid basis of good morals; therefore education should teach the precepts of religion and the duties of man towards God" and "the most important of all lessons [from the Bible] is the denunciation of ruin to every State that rejects the precepts of religion."

James McHenry, signer of the Constitution, said, "the Holy Scriptures ... can alone secure to society, order and peace, and to our courts of justice and constitutions of government, purity, stability, and usefulness. In vain, without the Bible, we increase penal laws and draw entrenchments around our institutions" and "Bibles are strong entrenchments. Where they abound, men cannot pursue wicked courses."

It is clear that the Founders of this nation, including those who wrote the Constitution, believed in and intended to create an

indissoluble union between the government of the United States of America and the principles of Christianity as revealed in the Holy Bible.

Whereas

On June 30, 1775, the Continental Congress passed its Articles of War which included this passage, "It is earnestly recommended to all officers and soldiers diligently to attend Divine service; and all officers and soldiers who shall behave indecently or irreverently at any place of Divine worship, shall … be brought before a court-martial."

On July 4, 1776, the Continental Congress approved a Declaration of Independence which proclaimed that "governments are instituted among men" in order "to secure these rights" which "are endowed by their Creator."

On July 4, 1776, the Continental Congress appointed a committee consisting of Benjamin Franklin, Thomas Jefferson, and John Adams to create a seal that would characterize the spirit on the newly proclaimed nation. Franklin proposed Moses lifting up his wand and dividing the Red Sea while Pharaoh and his charioteers were overwhelmed with the waters. He suggested this motto: "Rebellion to tyrants is obedience to God." Jefferson proposed the children of Israel guided through the wilderness by a pillar of cloud by day, and a pillar of fire by night.

On October 12, 1778, a Congressional resolution was passes which stated, "Whereas true religion and good morals are the only solid foundations of pubic liberty and happiness: Resolved, That it be, and it is hereby earnestly recommended to the several States to take the most effectual measures for the encouragement thereof."

On January 21, 1781, Robert Aitken asked the Congress for permission to print Bibles on his presses rather than import them from other countries. The Congress approved his request. Congress later approved the Bible which Mr. Aitken published. Inscribed in the front of that Bible was this endorsement: "Whereupon, Resolved, That the United States in Congress assembled … recommend this edition of the Bible to the inhabitants of the United States."

On August 7, 1789, President Washington signed into law the Northwest Ordinance, which had been previously enacted under the Articles of Confederation. This ordinance established the requirements of statehood for prospective new states. Article III states, "Religion, morality, and knowledge, being necessary to good government and the happiness of mankind, schools and the means of education shall forever be encouraged."

In 1789 the First Congress, which would also draft and approve the First Amendment, authorized the establishment of a chaplain for each house of Congress. These chaplains were paid with public funds and their duties included the responsibility to pray at the convening of each house of Congress. Congress also authorized the use of government buildings, including the Capitol building, to serve as houses of worship while awaiting the construction of churches in the national capital.

On September 25, 1789, Congress approved the Bill of Rights. Later that same day the following resolution was passed by Congress: "Resolved, That a joint committee of both Houses be directed to wait upon the President of the United States to request that he would recommend to the people of the United States a day of public thanksgiving and prayer, to be observed by acknowledging with grateful hearts the many signal favors of Almighty God, especially by affording them an opportunity peaceable to establish a Constitution of government for their safety and happiness...."

On October 3, 1789, President Washington – who had previously served as the president of the Constitutional Convention – issued the following Thanksgiving proclamation in response to the request from Congress, "Whereas it is the duty of all Nations to acknowledge the providence of Almighty God, to obey his will, to be grateful for his benefits, and humbly to implore his protection and favor...I do recommend and assign Thursday the 26th. day of November next to be devoted by the People of these States to the service of that great and glorious Being, who is the beneficent Author of all the good that was, that is, or that will be."

In 1853 a Report of the Senate Judiciary Committee stated, "They [the Founders] intended, by this [First] Amendment, to prohibit 'an establishment of religion' such as the English Church presented, or any thing like it. But they had no fear or jealousy of religion itself, nor did they wish to see us an irreligious people... they did not intend to spread over all the public authorities and the whole public action of the nation the dead and revolting spectacle of atheistical apathy."

In 1854 a Report of the House Judiciary Committee stated, "Had the people, during the Revolution, had a suspicion of any attempt to war against Christianity, that Revolution would have been strangled in its cradle. At the time of the adoption of the Constitution and the amendments, the universal sentiment was that Christianity should be encouraged, not any one sect. Any attempt to level and discard all religion would have been viewed with universal indignation.... It must be considered as the foundation on which the whole structure rests.... In this age there can be no substitute for Christianity; that, in its general principles, is the great conservative element on which we must rely for the purity and permanence of free institutions. That was the religion of the founders of the republic, and they expected it to remain the religion of their descendants."

It is clear that the Founders and first generations of Americans, as demonstrated in the acts of the Continental Congress and the Congress of the United States, believed in and intended to create an indissoluble union between the government of the United States of America and the principles of Christianity as revealed in the Holy Bible.

Whereas

John Jay, first Chief Justice of the United States Supreme Court, said it is "the duty of all wise, free, and virtuous governments to countenance and encourage virtue and religion" and "The Bible is the best of all books, for it is the word of God and teaches us the way to be happy in this world and in the next. Continue therefore to read it and to regulate your life by its precepts."

Oliver Ellsworth, third Chief Justice of the United States Supreme Court, said, "the primary objects of government, are peace, order, and prosperity of society.... To the promotion of these objects, ... good morals are essential. Institutions for the promotion of good morals are, therefore, objects of legislative provision and support: and among these ... religious institutions are eminently useful and important.... The legislature, charged with the great interests of the community, may, and ought to countenance, aid, and protect religious institutions ... the legislature may aid the maintenance of [Christianity], whose benign influence on morals is universally acknowledged. It may be added that this principle has been long recognized, and is too intimately connected with the peace, order, and happiness of the state to be abandoned."

William Paterson, signer of the Constitution and United States Supreme Court Justice, said, "Religion and morality ... [are] necessary to good government, good order, and good laws."

James Wilson, signer of the Constitution and United States Supreme Court Justice, said, "All [laws], however, may be arranged in two different classes. 1) Divine. 2) Human. ... But it should always be remembered that this law, natural or revealed, made for men or for nations, flows from the same Divine source: it is the law of God.... Human law must rest its authority ultimately upon the authority of that law which is Divine."

Joseph Story, founder of the Harvard School of Law, author of the legal classic *Commentaries on the Constitution of the United States*, and United States Supreme Court Justice said about the First Amendment, "We are not to attribute this prohibition of a national religious establishment to an indifference to religion in general, and especially to Christianity, which none could hold in more reverence than the framers of the Constitution.... Indeed, the right of a society or government to [participate] in matters of religion will hardly be contested by any persons who believe that piety, religion, and morality are intimately connected with the well being of the state and indispensable to the administration of civil justice.... It is, indeed, difficult to conceive how any civilized society can well exist without them. And, at all events, it is impossible for those who believe in the truth of Christianity as a Divine revelation to doubt that it is the especial duty of government to foster and encourage it among all the citizens and subjects...." and "Probably, at the time of the adoption of the Constitution, and of the Amendment to it now under consideration, the general, if not the universal, sentiment in America was that Christianity ought to receive encouragement from the State.... An attempt to level all religions and to make it a matter of state policy to hold all in utter indifference would have created universal disapprobation if not universal indignation" and "One of the beautiful boasts of our municipal jurisprudence is that Christianity is a part of the Common Law.... There never has been a period in which the Common Law did not recognize Christianity as lying at its foundations.... I verily believe Christianity necessary to the support of civil society."

It is clear that the Founders of this nation, including those who served as Justices of the United States Supreme Court, believed

in and intended to create an indissoluble union between the government of the United States of America and the principles of Christianity as revealed in the Holy Bible.

Whereas

In *Vidal v. Girard's Executors* (1844) the United States Supreme Court stated,

"It is also said, and truly, that the Christian religion is a part of the common law."

In *City of Charleston v. S. A. Benjamin* (1846) the United States Supreme Court stated,

"Christianity is a part of the common law of the land, with liberty of conscience to all. It has always been so recognized.... If Christianity is a part of the common law, its disturbance is punishable at common law. The U. S. Constitution allows it as a part of the common law... Christianity is part and parcel of the common law.... Christianity has reference to the principles of right and wrong ... it is the foundation of those morals and manners upon which our society is formed; it is their basis. Remove this and they would fall....What constitutes the standard of good morals? Is it not Christianity? There certainly is none other ... the day of moral virtue in which we live would, in an instant, if that standard were abolished, lapse into the dark and murky night of Pagan immorality. In the Courts over which we preside, we daily acknowledge Christianity as the most solemn part of our administration."

In *The Church of the Holy Trinity v. United States* (1892) the United States Supreme Court stated, "This is historically true. From the discovery of this continent to the present hour, there is a single voice making this affirmation ... There is no dissonance in these declarations. There is a universal language pervading them all, having one meaning; they affirm and reaffirm that this is a religious nation. These are not individual sayings, declarations of private persons: they are organic utterances; they speak the voice of the entire people ... These and many other matters which might be noticed, add a volume of unofficial declarations to the mass of organic utterances that this is a Christian nation."

In *United States v. Macintosh* (1931) the United States Supreme Court stated, "We are a Christian people ... according to one another the equal right of religious freedom and acknowledging with reverence the duty of obedience to the will of God."

In *Zorach v. Clauson* (1952) the United States Supreme Court stated, "We are a religious people whose institutions presuppose a Supreme Being.... When the State encourages religious instruction or cooperates with religious authorities by adjusting the schedule of public events to sectarian needs, if follows the best of our traditions. For it then respects the religious nature of our people and accommodates the public service to their spiritual needs. To hold that it may not would be to find in the Constitution a requirement that the government show a callous indifference to religious groups. That would be preferring those who believe in no religion over those who do believe.... [W]e find no constitutional requirement which makes it necessary for government to be hostile to religion and to throw its weight against efforts to widen the effective scope of religious influence."

In *Everson v. Board of Education* (1947) the United States Supreme Court first erected the "wall of separation between church and state" as a principle for basing its rulings; but, as we have seen from the preceding evidence, that principle is not consistent with the original intent of the Founders nor the Constitution. In *Wallace v. Jaffree* (1985) Chief Justice William Rehnquist filed this complaint: "There is simply no historical foundation for the proposition that the Framers intended to build the 'wall of separation' that was constitutionalized in *Everson*.... But the greatest injury of the 'wall' notion is its mischievous diversion of judges from the actual intentions of the drafters of the Bill of Rights.... no amount of repetition of historical errors in judicial opinions can make the errors true. The 'wall of separation between church and State' is a metaphor based on bad history.... It should be frankly and explicitly abandoned.... Our perception has been clouded not by the Constitution but by the mists of an unnecessary metaphor."

It is clear that until recently the United States Supreme Court consistently upheld the belief that the Founders and the Constitution intended to create an indissoluble union between the government of the United States of America and the principles of Christianity as revealed in the Holy Bible.

Therefore be it resolved that this school district intends to honor the heritage of the United States and the legal intent of the

Founders and the Constitution by enacting these ordinances to apply throughout this school district:

(1) Voluntary, non-denominational prayer shall be allowed at all school functions and at all school facilities, and

(2) Images of the Ten Commandments and the text of the Ten Commandments shall be allowed at all school functions and at all school facilities, and

(3) The moral lessons expressed in the Ten Commandments shall be taught in each elementary school class and in every language and civics class in grades six through twelve.

APPENDIX C:

HOMELESS ACTION PLAN

Establish a leadership board consisting of volunteers from various church, synagogue, and charitable organizations as described in Appendix A.

Meet and work with representatives from the local mayor's office.

Find an unused property that would be suitable for short-term housing. A closed motel would be ideal. A large warehouse would also be suitable. Work with the city to arrange with the property owner / manager for the use of the property. Renovate the property to allow for sleeping quarters, bathroom and shower facilities, classrooms, communal areas for meetings, and security.

Coordinate with police and other city officials to bring homeless to the housing facility.

Screen the potential residents to place them in appropriate categories; for example, drug and alcohol addicts, mental health candidates, those with a criminal record, and those with health requirements.

Assign volunteers to each resident to work with them to help in their rehabilitation.

Develop a group of volunteers who can provide useful training to the residents designed to give them the rehabilitation and instruction necessary for them to return to a productive, independent life.

Arrange with local food service businesses (grocery stores, restaurants, bakeries, etc.) to donate food for the homeless residents. Establish a group of volunteers who will regularly collect this food from these food service businesses.

Establish a security force to maintain order and safety at the residence. Volunteers with a law-enforcement background would be ideal.

Establish a daily routine for the residents consisting of meals, spiritual development, classes, training, maintenance of the property, physical fitness, and where possible, using residents to help each other.

Work with local government to look for activities designed to allow residents to help the community; for example, trash pickup, gardening, simple maintenance jobs, etc.

Coordinate with employment services to locate work for the residents who have developed the skills necessary for particular jobs.

Provide counselors who will direct the residents progress while residing at the property and monitor their progress after leaving the residence.

Provide low-cost housing counseling to prepare for the time when the residents can move out of the shelter and into their own homes.

Recognize and reward residents as they make progress and achieve various levels of improvement.